HOW TO INSTANTLY

SPEAK Spanish ON THE Job

THOUSANDS OF TRANSLATED WORDS

AND PHRASES SPECIALIZED FOR:

- CONSTRUCTION
- LANDSCAPING
- HOUSEKEEPING
- RESTAURANTS
- HOME & BUILDING MAINTENANCE

Speak Spanish in just sec...

Published by Southwestern Press, Inc.
P.O. Box 4297, Carlsbad, California 92018
Tel. (760) 434-8858 | www.SouthwesternPress.com

Please send comments or suggestions to Comments@SouthwesternPress.com

---

Library of Congress Control Number: 2007905553

ISBN-13 978-0-923176-11-2

LIMIT OF LIABILITY AND DISCLAIMER OF WARRANTY: EVERY EFFORT HAS BEEN MADE TO MAKE THIS BOOK AS COMPLETE AND ACCURATE AS POSSIBLE, BUT NO WARRANTY OR FITNESS IS IMPLIED. THE INFORMATION PROVIDED IS ON AN "AS IS" BASIS. THE AUTHOR AND THE PUBLISHER SHALL HAVE NEITHER LIABILITY NOR RESPONSIBILITY TO ANY PERSON OR ENTITY WITH RESPECT TO ANY LOSS OR DAMAGES ARISING FROM THE INFORMATION CONTAINED IN THIS BOOK.

THIS PUBLICATION CONTAINS THE OPINIONS AND IDEAS OF ITS AUTHORS. IT IS INTENDED TO PROVIDE HELPFUL AND INFORMATIVE MATERIAL ON THE SUBJECT COVERED. IT IS SOLD WITH THE UNDERSTANDING THAT THE AUTHOR AND PUBLISHER ARE NOT ENGAGED IN RENDERING PROFESSIONAL SERVICES IN THE BOOK. IF THE READER REQUIRES PERSONAL ASSISTANCE OR ADVICE, A COMPETENT PROFESSIONAL SHOULD BE CONSULTED.

THE AUTHOR AND PUBLISHER SPECIFICALLY DISCLAIM ANY RESPONSIBILITY FOR ANY LIABILITY, LOSS OR RISK, PERSONAL OR OTHERWISE, WHICH IS INCURRED AS A CONSEQUENCE, DIRECTLY OR INDIRECTLY, OF THE USE AND APPLICATION OF ANY CONTENTS OF THIS BOOK.

LÍMITE DE RESPONSABILIDAD Y EXCLUSIÓN DE GARANTÍAS: EL AUTOR Y LA CASA EDITORA, SOUTHWESTERN PRESS INC., NO SERÁN RESPONSABLES ANTE NINGUNA PERSONA O ENTIDAD EN RELACIÓN CON CUALQUIER PÉRDIDA O POR DAÑOS Y PERJUICIOS QUE SURJAN DE LA INFORMACIÓN CONTENIDA EN ESTOS LIBROS.

LA INFORMACIÓN PROPORCIONADA TIENE LA INTENCIÓN DE PROPORCIONAR MATERIAL ÚTIL E INFORMATIVO SOBRE EL TEMA CUBIERTO PERO LOS LIBROS SON VENDIDOS EN BASE "TAL COMO SON". SE HA HECHO TODO ESFUERZO PARA QUE ESTOS LIBROS SEAN TAN COMPLETOS Y PRECISOS COMO SEA POSIBLE, PERO NO ASUMIMOS NINGUNA GARANTÍA O ADECUACIÓN IMPLÍCITA PARA UN FIN O USO DETERMINADO.

ESTAS PUBLICACIONES CONTIENEN OPINIONES E IDEAS Y SE VENDEN EN EL ENTENDIDO DE QUE LA CASA EDITORA NO ESTÁ DEDICADA A PROPORCIONAR SERVICIOS PROFESIONALES A TRAVÉS DE ESTOS LIBROS. SI EL LECTOR REQUIERE AYUDA PROFESIONAL Y/O ASESORÍA, DEBE PONERSE EN CONTACTO CON UN PROFESIONAL COMPETENTE.

SOUTHWESTERN PRESS INC. ESPECÍFICAMENTE RENUNCIA A TODA RESPONSABILIDAD, PÉRDIDA, O RIESGO, TANTO PERSONAL COMO DE OTRO TIPO EN QUE SE INCURRA COMO CONSECUENCIA, DIRECTA O INDIRECTAMENTE, DEL USO Y DE LA APLICACIÓN DE CUALQUIER PARTE DEL CONTENIDO DE ESTOS LIBROS.

Introduction

If you don't speak Spanish, but need to quickly communicate with a Spanish-speaking worker, what do you do?

Use **Speak Spanish on the Job**—the quick and easy translation guide!

This handy, pocket-sized book uses phonetics to show you how to pronounce each word or phrase. This means you have the <u>instant</u> ability to speak common employment-based Spanish.

The simple, straightforward layout of this book helps speed communication for anyone, but especially for those working in construction, landscaping, housekeeping, restaurants, and building or home maintenance.

Speak Spanish in just seconds!

Table of Contents

Useful phrases / Frases útiles

Useful phrases	Frases útiles
Are you hungry?	**¿Tiene hambre?** tee-EH-neh ahm-BREH
Are you okay?	**¿Está bien?** es-TAH be-EN
Are you sick?	**¿Está enfermo?** es-TAH en-fehr-MOH
Be careful.	**Tenga cuidado.** TEN-gah kwee-DAH-doh
Be here at ___.	**Esté aquí a ___.*** es-TEH ah-KEE ah ___
Call me, please.	**Llámeme, por favor.** YAH-meh-meh, por fah-VOR
Can you read?	**¿Sabe leer?** SAH-beh leh-EHR
Can you work on ___?	**¿Puede trabajar el ___?†** PWEH-deh trah-bah-HAR el ___
Can you write?	**¿Sabe escribir?** SAH-beh es-kree-BEER
Do it like this.	**Hágalo así.** AH-gah-loh ah-SEE

*Time page 26 †Days page 22

Do the job right the first time, please.	**Haga bien el trabajo la primera vez, por favor.** AH-gah be-en el trah-BAH-ho lah pree-MEH-rah ves, por fah-VOR
Do you have a driver's license?	**¿Tiene una licencia de manejar?** tee-EH-neh OO-nah lee-SEN-see-ah deh mah-neh-HAR
Do you have any questions?	**¿Tiene algunas preguntas?** tee-EH-neh ahl-GOO-nahs preh-goon-TAHS
Do you have a Social Security card?	**¿Tiene una tarjeta de Seguro Social?** tee-EH-neh OO-nah tar-HEH-tah deh seh-GOO-roh soh-see-AHL
Do you have experience?	**¿Tiene experiencia?** tee-EH-neh eks-peh-ree-en-see-AH
Do you have friends who want to work?	**¿Tiene amigos que quieran trabajar?** tee-EH-neh ah-MEE-gohs keh kee-EH-rahn trah-bah-HAR
Do you have papers to work?	**¿Tiene papeles para trabajar?** tee-EH-neh pah-PEH-les PAH-rah trah-bah-HAR
Do you have references?	**¿Tiene referencias?** tee-EH-neh reh-feh-ren-see-AHS
Do you know how to ___?	**¿Sabe cómo ___?*** SAH-beh KOH-moh ___
Do you need medical care?	**¿Necesita tratamiento médico?** neh-seh-SEE-tah trah-tah-mee-EN-toh meh-dee-KOH

*Useful Terms page 28

Do you speak English?	**¿Habla inglés?**	
	AH-blah een-GLEHS	

Do you understand?	**¿Entiende?**	
	en-tee-en-DEH	

Do you want ___?	**¿Quiere ___?***	
	kee-EH-reh ___	

Do you want to work?	**¿Quiere trabajar?**	
	kee-EH-reh trah bah-HAR	

Good afternoon.	**Buenas tardes.**	
	BWEH-nahs TAR-des	

Good bye.	**Adiós.**	
	ah-dee-OHS	

Good evening.	**Buenas noches.**	
	BWEH-nahs NOH-chehs	

Good job!	**¡Buen trabajo!**	
	bwen trah-BAH-ho	

Good morning.	**Buenos días.**	
	BWEH-nohs DEE-ahs	

Good, thank you.	**Bien gracias.**	
	bc-en GRAH-see-ahs	

How are you?	**¿Cómo está usted?**	
	KOH-moh es-TAH oo-STED	

*Useful Terms page 28

How do you say ___?	**¿Cómo se dice ___?** KOH-moh seh DEE-seh ___
How many?	**¿Cuántos?** KWAN-tohs
How much?	**¿Cuánto?** KWAN-toh
How old are you?	**¿Cuántos años tiene?** KWAN-tohs AH-nyos tee-EH-neh
Hurry up!	**¡Apúrese!** ah-POO-reh-seh
I don't understand.	**No entiendo.** noh en-tee-EN-doh
I have another job for you.	**Tengo otro trabajo para usted.** TEN-goh OH-troh trah-BAH-ho PAH-rah oo-STED
I'll be back in ___ day(s).	**Volveré en ___ día(s).*** vol-veh-REH en ___ DEE-ah(s)
I'll be back in ___ hour(s).	**Volveré en ___ hora(s).*** vol-veh-REH en ___ OH-rah(s)
I'll be back in ___ minute(s).	**Volveré en ___ minuto(s).*** vol-veh-REH en ___ mee-NU-toh(s)
I'll be back in ___ week(s).	**Volveré en ___ semana(s).*** vol-veh-REH en ___ seh-MAH-nah(s)

*Numbers page 18

I'll pick you up.	**Pásare por usted.** PAH-sah-reh por oo-STED
Is there a problem?	**¿Hay algún problema?** I ahl-GOON proh-bleh-MAH
Let me know when you are finished.	**Avíseme cuando haya terminado.** ah-VEE-seh-meh KWAHN-doh AH-yah tehr-mee-NAH-doh
Listen carefully please.	**Por favor, escuche con cuidado.** por fah-VOR, es-KOO-cheh kohn kwee-DAH-doh
Look out!	**¡Cuidado!** kwee-DAH-doh
May I please speak with ___?	**Por favor, ¿puedo hablar con ___?** por fah-VOR, PWEH-doh ah-BLAR kohn ___
My address is ___.	**Mi dirección es ___.*** mee dee-rek-see-OHN es ___
My name is ___.	**Me llamo ___.** meh YAH-moh ___
	Mi nombre es ___. mee NOHM-breh es ___
My phone number is ___.	**Mi número de teléfono es ___.*** mee NU-meh-roh deh teh-LEH-foh-noh es ___

Please have him/her call me.	**Dígale que me llame, por favor.** DEE-gah-leh keh meh YAH-meh, por fah-VOR
Please speak slower.	**Por favor hable más despacio.** por fah-VOR AH-bleh MAHS des-PAH-see-oh
Repeat that, please.	**Repítalo que dijo, por favor.** reh-pee-TAH-loh keh DEE-ho, por fah-VOR
Show me, please. (license, papers, card)	**Muéstrame, por favor** MWEHS-trah-meh, por fah-VOR
Start work at ___ .	**Empiece a trabajar a ___ .*** em-pee-EH-seh ah trah-bah-HAR ah ___
Take a break.	**Tome un descanso.** TOH-meh oon des-KAHN-soh
That is all for today.	**Esto es todo por hoy.** ES-toh es TOH-doh por oy
That's good.	**Está bien.** es-TAH be-en
This is ___ . May I please speak with ___ .	**Soy ___ . Por favor, ¿puedo hablar con ___ ?** soy ___ por fah-VOR, PWEH-doh ah-BLAR kohn ___
This is the last time.	**Esta es la última vez.** ES-tah es lah OOL-tee-mah ves
Very well, thank you.	**Muy bien, gracias.** moo-EE be-en, GRAH-see-ahs

*Time page 26

Wait here.	**Espere aquí.** es-PEH-reh ah-KEE
Watch out!	**¡Cuidado!** kwee-DAH-doh
What?	**¿Qué?** keh
What do you call this?	**¿Cómo le dice usted a esto?** KOH-moh leh DEE-seh oo-STED ah ES-toh
What is this?	**¿Qué es esto?** KEH es ES-toh
What is your address?	**¿Cuál es su dirección?** kwahl es su dee-rek-see-OHN
What is your last name?	**¿Cómo se apellida?** KOH-moh seh ah-peh-YEE-dah
What is your name?	**¿Cómo se llama?** KOH moh seh YAH-mah
What is your Social Security number?	**¿Cuál es su número de Seguro Social?** kwahl es su NU-meh-roh deh seh-GOO-roh soh-see-AHL
What is your telephone number?	**¿Cuál es su número de teléfono?** kwahl es su NU-meh-roh deh teh-LEH-foh-noh
When?	**¿Cuándo?** KWAN-doh

Where?	**¿Dónde?** DOHN-deh
Where do you work and what do you do?	**¿Dónde trabaja usted y cuál es su oficio?** DOHN-deh trah-BAH-ha oo-STED ee kwahl es su oh-FEE-see-oh
Who?	**¿Quién?** kee-EN
Why?	**¿Por qué?** por KEH
You can't work because you are sick.	**No puede trabajar porque está enfermo.** noh PWEH-deh trah-bah-HAR POR-keh es-TAH en-FEHR-moh
You're early.	**Usted llegó temprano.** oo-STED yeh-GOH tehm-PRAH-noh
You're fired.	**Usted está despedido.** oo-STED es-TAH des-peh-DEE-doh
You're hired.	**Usted está contratado.** oo-STED es-TAH kohn-trah-TAH-doh
You're late.	**Usted llegó tarde.** oo-STED yeh-GOH TAR-deh
You're welcome.	**De nada.** deh NAH-dah
	No hay de qué. no I deh keh

Money   Dinero

bonus	**pago extraordinario** PAH-goh eks-trah-or-dee-NAH-ree-oh
cash	**efectivo** eh-fek-TEE-voh
charge (to) (a price/fee)	**cobrar** koh-BRAR
check(s)	**cheque(s)** CHEH-keh(s)
dollar(s)	**dólar(es)** DOH-lar-(es)
minimum wage	**salario mínimo** sah-LAH-ree-oh MEE-nee-moh
money order(s)	**giro(s) postal(es)** HEE-roh(s) pohs-TAHL-(es)
overtime pay	**pago extra por horas extras** PAH-goh EKS-trah por OH-rahs EKS-trahs
pay (to)	**pagar** pah-GAR
pay day	**día de pago** DEE-ah deh PAH-goh
plus room and board	**más el cuarto y comida** mahs el KWAR-toh ee koh-MEE-dah
tips	**propinas** proh-PEE-nahs

Payment Pago

| Can I pay you in cash? | ¿Puedo pagarle en efectivo? |
| | PWEH-doh pah-GAR-leh en eh-fek-tee-VOH |

| Can I pay you with a check? | ¿Puedo pagarle con un cheque? |
| | PWEH-doh pah-GAR-leh kohn oon cheh-KEH |

| Do you need an advance? | ¿Necesita un anticipo? |
| | neh-seh-SEE-tah oon ahn-tee-see-POH |

| Do you need money? | ¿Necesita dinero? |
| | neh-seh-SEE-tah dee-neh-ROH |

| How much? | ¿Cuánto? |
| | KWAHN-toh |

| How much do you charge? | ¿Cuánto cobra usted? |
| | KWAHN-toh KOH-brah oo-STED |

| I pay every ___. | Pago cada ___.† |
| | KWAHN-toh KOH-brah oo-STED ___ |

| I will pay you ___. | Le pagaré el ___.† |
| | leh pah-gah-REH el ___ |

| The pay week ends on ___. | La semana de pago termina en ___.† |
| | lah seh-MAH-nah deh PAH-go tehr-MEE-nah en ___ |

| I charge . . . | Cobro |
| | KOH-broh |

| I pay . . . | Pago |
| | PAH-goh |

| We charge . . . | Cobramos |
| | koh-BRAH-mohs |

†Days page 22

| We pay . . . | **Pagamos** |
| | pah-GAH-mohs |

| You charge . . . | **Cobre** |
| | KOH-breh |

| You pay . . . | **Pague** |
| | PAH-geh |

| . . . $ ___.00 an hour. | **$ ___ dólares la hora.*** |
| | $ ___ DOH-lah-res lah OH-rah |

. . . $ ___.25 an hour.	**$ ___ dólares y veinticinco centavos la hora.***
	$ ___ DOH-lah-res ee vein-tee-SEEN-koh
	sen-TAH-vohs lah OH-rah

. . . $ ___.50 an hour.	**$ ___ dólares y cincuenta centavos la hora.***
	$ ___ DOH-lah-res ee seen-KWEN-tah
	sen-TAH-vohs lah OH-rah

. . . $ ___.75 an hour.	**$ ___ dólares y setenta y cinco centavos la hora.***
	$ ___ DOH-lah-res ee seh-TEN-tah ee
	SEEN-koh sen-TAH-vohs lah OH-rah

| . . . $ ___ a day. | **$ ___ dólares el día.*** |
| | $ ___ DOH-lah-res el DEE-ah |

| . . . $ ___ a week. | **$ ___ dólares la semana.*** |
| | $ ___ DOH-lah-res lah seh-MAH-nah |

| . . . $ ___ a month. | **$ ___ dólares el mes.*** |
| | $ ___ DOH-lah-res el mehs |

*Numbers page 18

Numbers   Numeros

0	**cero** SEH-roh
1	**uno** OO-noh
2	**dos** dohs
3	**tres** trehs
4	**cuatro** KWAH-troh
5	**cinco** SEEN-koh
6	**seis** sase
7	**siete** see-EH-teh
8	**ocho** OH-cho
9	**nueve** NWEH-veh
10	**diez** dee-es
11	**once** OHN-seh
12	**doce** DOH-seh
13	**trece** TREH-seh

14	**catorce** kah-TOR-seh
15	**quince** KEEN-seh
16	**dieciséis** dee-es-ee-SEH-ees
17	**diecisiete** dee-es-ee-see-EH-teh
18	**dieciocho** dee-es-ee-OH-cho
19	**diecinueve** dee-es-ee-NWEH-veh
20	**veinte** VEIN-teh
21	**veinte y uno** VEIN-teh ee OO-noh
22	**veinte y dos** VEIN-teh ee dohs
30	**treinta** TREIN-tah
40	**cuarenta** kwah-REN-tah
50	**cincuenta** seen-KWEN-tah
55	**cincuenta y cinco** seen-KWEN-tah ee SEEN-koh
60	**sesenta** seh-SEN-tah
70	**setenta** seh-TEN-tah

80	**ochenta**	oh-CHEN-tah
90	**noventa**	noh-VEN-tah
100	**cien**	see-en
150	**ciento cincuenta**	see-EN-toh seen-KWEN-tah
200	**doscientos**	dohs-see-EN-tohs
300	**trescientos**	trehs-see-EN-tohs
400	**cuatrocientos**	kwah-troh-see-EN-tohs
500	**quinientos**	kee-nee-EN-tohs
600	**seiscientos**	sase-see-EN-tohs
700	**setecientos**	seh-teh-see-EN-tohs
800	**ochocientos**	oh-cho-see-EN-tohs
900	**novecientos**	noh-veh-see-EN-tohs
1000	**mil**	meel

Ordinal numbers

Números ordinales

first	**primero**
	pree-MEH-roh
second	**segundo**
	seh-GOON-doh
third	**tercero**
	tehr-SEH-roh
fourth	**cuarto**
	KWAR-toh
fifth	**quinto**
	KEEN-toh
sixth	**sexto**
	SEKS-toh
seventh	**séptimo**
	SEP-tee-moh
eighth	**octavo**
	ohk TAH-voh
ninth	**noveno**
	noh-VEH-noh
tenth	**décimo**
	DEH-see-moh

Days	Días
Sunday	**domingo** doh-MEEN-goh
Monday	**lunes** LOO-nes
Tuesday	**martes** MAR-tes
Wednesday	**miércoles** mee-EHR-koh-les
Thursday	**jueves** HWEH-ves
Friday	**viernes** vee-EHR-nes
Saturday	**sábado** SAH-bah-doh

Can you work on ___?	**¿Puede trabajar el ___?** PWEH-deh trah-bah-HAR el ___
I pay every ___.	**Pago cada ___.** PAH-goh KAH-dah ___
I will pay you on ___.	**Le pagaré el ___.** leh pah-gah-REH el ___
The pay week ends on ___.	**La semana de pago termina en ___.** lah seh-MAH-nah deh PAH-go tehr-MEE-nah en ___
You will have ___ off.	**Descansará el ___.** des-kahn-sah-RAH el ___
You will work ___.	**Va a trabajar ___.** vah ah trah-ba-HAR ___

Months	Meses
January	**enero** eh-NEH-roh
February	**febrero** feh-BREH-roh
March	**marzo** MAR-soh
April	**abril** ah-BREEL
May	**mayo** MAH-yoh
June	**junio** HOO-nee-oh
July	**julio** HOO-lee-oh
August	**agosto** ah-GOHS-toh
September	**septiembre** sep-tee-EM-breh
October	**octubre** ohk-TOO-breh
November	**noviembre** noh-vee-EM-breh
December	**diciembre** dee-see-EM-breh

Expressions of time
Expresiones de tiempo

afternoon(s)	**tarde(s)** TAR-deh(s)
all day	**todo el día** TOH-doh el DEE-ah
all the time	**todo el tiempo** TOH-doh el tee-EM-poh
at night	**por la noche** por lah NOH-cheh
daily/everyday	**todos los días** TOH-dohs lohs DEE-ahs
day(s)	**día(s)** DEE-ah(s)
hour(s)	**hora(s)** OH-rah(s)
in the morning	**por la mañana** por lah mah-NYAH-nah
last night	**anoche** ah-NOH-cheh
last week	**semana pasada** seh-MAH-nah pah-SAH-dah
later (afterwards)	**después** des-PWEHS
midnight	**medianoche** meh-dee-ah-NOH-cheh
minute(s)	**minuto(s)** mee-NU-toh(s)

month(s)	**mes(es)**	
	MEHS-(es)	
morning(s)	**mañana(s)**	
	mah-NYAH-nah(s)	
next	**próximo**	
	PROK-see-moh	
next week	**semana próxima**	
	seh-MAH-nah PROK-see-mah	
night(s)	**noche(s)**	
	NOH-cheh(s)	
noon	**mediodía**	
	meh-dee-oh-DEE-ah	
now	**ahora**	
	ah-OH-rah	
second(s)	**segundo(s)**	
	seh-GOON-doh(s)	
today	**hoy**	
	oy	
tomorrow	**mañana**	
	mah-NYAH-nah	
tonight	**esta noche**	
	ES-tah NOH-cheh	
week(s)	**semana(s)**	
	seh-MAH-nah(s)	
weekend(s)	**fin(es) de semana**	
	FEEN-(es) deh seh-MAH-nah	
year(s)	**año(s)**	
	AH-nyoh(s)	
yesterday	**ayer**	
	ah-YEHR	

Time

Tiempo

| Be here at ___. | Esté aquí a ___. |
| | es-TEH ah-KEE ah ___ |

| I'll be back at ___. | Volveré a ___. |
| | vol-veh-REH ah ___ |

| I'll pick you up at ___. | Pásare por usted a ___. |
| | PAH-sah-reh por oo-STED ah ___ |

| | Lo recogeré a ___. |
| | loh reh-koh-heh-REH ah ___ |

| Quit/stop work at ___. | Deje de trabajar a ___. |
| | DEH-heh deh trah-bah-HAR ah ___ |

| Start work at ___. | Empiece a trabajar a ___. |
| | em-pee-EH-seh ah trah-bah-HAR ah ___ |

| Take a break at ___. | Tome un descanso a ___. |
| | TOH-meh oon des-KAHN-soh ah ___ |

| What time is it? | ¿Qué hora es? |
| | keh OH-rah ehs |

| You may leave at ___. | Se puede ir a ___. |
| | seh PWEH-deh eer ah ___ |

| 1:00 | la una |
| | lah OO-nah |

| 1:15 | la una y cuarto |
| | lah OO-nah ee KWAR-toh |

1:30	**la una y media** lah OO-nah ee MEH-dee-ah	
1:45	**la una y cuarenta y cinco** lah OO-nah ee kwah-REN-tah ee SEEN-koh	
2:00	**las dos** lahs dohs	
3:00	**las tres** lahs trehs	
4:00	**las cuatro** lahs KWAH-troh	
5:00	**las cinco** lahs SEEN-koh	
6:00	**las seis** lahs sase	
7:00	**las siete** lahs sec-EH-teh	
8:00	**las ocho** lahs OH-cho	
9:00	**las nueve** lahs NWEH-veh	
10:00	**las diez** lahs dee-ES	
11:00	**las once** lahs OHN-seh	
12:00	**las doce** lahs DOH-seh	

Useful terms	Términos útiles
above (over)	**encima de** en-SEE-mah deh
	sobre SOH-breh
	por encima por en-SEE-mah
above (overhead)	**arriba** ah-REE-bah
abuse(s)	**abuso(s)** ah-BOO-soh(s)
accident(s)	**accidente(s)** ahk-see-DEN-teh(s)
acid/acidic	**ácido** AH-see-doh
across	**a través** ah trah-VEHS
acrylic	**acrílico** ah-KREE-lee-koh
adapter(s)	**adaptador(es)** ah-dahp-tah-DOR-(es)
add (to)	**agregar** ah-greh-GAR
add (to) (numbers)	**sumar** su-MAR
address(es)	**dirección (direcciones)** dee-rek-see-OHN (dee-rek-see-OH-nes)

adhesive	**adhesivo** odd-eh-SEE-voh
adjustable wrench (monkey wrench)	**llave inglesa** YAH-veh een-GLEH-sah
aerate the lawn (to)	**airear el césped** i-reh-AR el SEHS-ped
after (later)	**después** des-PWEHS
afternoon(s)	**tarde(s)** TAR-deh(s)
again	**otra vez** OH-trah ves
	de nuevo deh NWEH-voh
agriculture	**agricultura** ah-gree-kool-TOO-rah
air	**aire** I-reh
air compressor(s)	**compresor(es) de aire** kohm-preh-SOR-(es) deh I-reh
air conditioner(s)	**acondicionador(es) de aire** ah-kohn-dee-see-oh-nah-DOR-(es) deh I-reh
air filter(s)	**filtro(s) de aire** FEEL-troh(s) deh I-reh
air hose(s)	**manguera(s) de aire** mahn-GEH-rah(s) deh I-reh
alarm(s)	**alarma(s)** ah-LAR-mah(s)
alkaline	**alcalino** ahl-kah-LEE-noh

all (everything)	**todo** TOH-doh
allen wrench	**llave hexagonal** YAH-veh eks-ah-goh-NAHL
	llave allen YAH-veh AH-len
all the time	**todo el tiempo** TOH-doh el tee-EM-poh
aluminum	**aluminio** ah-loo-MEE-nee-oh
aluminum foil	**papel de aluminio** pah-PEL deh ah-loo-MEE-nee-oh
always	**siempre** see-EM-preh
ambulance(s)	**ambulancia(s)** ahm-boo-LAHN-see-ah(s)
amendments (soil)	**corrección de suelos** koh-rek-see-OHN deh SWEH-lohs
	enmiendas de suelos en-mee-EN-dahs deh SWEH-lohs
anchor bolt(s)	**perno(s) de anclaje** PEHR-noh(s) deh ahn-KLAH-heh
and	**y** ee
angle(s)	**ángulo(s)** AHN-goo-loh(s)
animal(s)	**animal(es)** ah-nee-MAHL-(es)
ankle(s)	**tobillo(s)** toh-BEE-yoh(s)

annual	**anual**
	ahn-WAHL
ant(s)	**hormiga(s)**
	or-MEE-gah(s)
ant bait	**cebo para hormigas**
	SEH-boh PAH-rah or-MEE-gahs
ant colony	**colonia de hormigas**
	koh-LOH-nee-ah deh or-MEE-gahs
ant trap(s)	**trampa(s) de cebo para hormigas**
	TRAHM-pah(s) deh SEH-boh PAH-rah or-MEE-gahs
aphid(s)	**áfido(s)**
	AH-fee-doh(s)
	pulgón (pulgones)
	pool-GOHN (pool-GOH-nes)
apple(s)	**manzana(s)**
	mahn-SAH-nah(s)
applicator(s)	**aplicador(es)**
	ah-plee-kah-DOR-(es)
apply (to put on)	**aplicar**
	ah-plee-KAR
apply (you put on)	**aplique**
	ah-PLEE-keh
apricot(s)	**chabacano(s)**
	cha-bah-KAH-noh(s)
	albaricoque(s)
	ahl-bah-ree-KOH-keh(s)
	damasco(s)
	dah-MAHS-koh(s)
April	**abril**
	ah-BREEL

apron(s)	**delantal(es)** deh-lahn-TAHL-(es)
	mandil(es) mahn-DEEL-(es)
arch(es)	**arco(s)** AR-koh(s)
area(s)	**área(s)** AH-reh-ah(s)
arm(s)	**brazo(s)** BRAH-soh(s)
armchair(s)	**sillón (sillones)** see-YOHN (see-YOH-nes)
ash(es)	**ceniza(s)** seh-NEE-sah(s)
ashtray(s)	**cenicero(s)** seh-nee-SEH-roh(s)
asleep	**dormido** dor-MEE-doh
asphalt	**asfalto** ahs-FAHL-toh
aspirin	**aspirina** ahs-pee-REE-nah
assemble (to)	**ensamblar** en-sahm-BLAR
	montar mohn-TAR
assemble (you)	**ensamble** en-SAHM-bleh
	monte MOHN-teh

attach (to)	**sujetar** su-heh-TAR
	fijar fee-HAR
	pegar peh-GAR
attic(s)	**ático(s)** AH-tee-koh(s)
auger(s)	**barrena(s)** bah-REH-nah(s)
August	**agosto** ah-GOHS-toh
aunt(s)	**tía(s)** TEE-ah(s)
automatic	**automático** ow-toh-MAH-tee-koh
auto mechanic	**mecánico de automóviles** meh-KAH-nee-koh deh ow-toh-MOH-veel-es
automobile(s)	**automóvil(es)** ow-toh-MOH-veel-(es)
avocado(s)	**aguacate(s)** ah-gwah-KAH-teh(s)
avoid (to)	**evitar** eh-vee-TAR
awake	**despierto** des-pee-EHR-toh
axe(s)	**hacha(s)** AH-cha(s)

baby bottle(s)	**biberón (biberones)**	
	bee-beh-ROHN (bee-beh-ROH-nes)	
	botella(s)	
	boh-TEH-yah(s)	
back	**atrás**	
	ah-TRAHS	
	detrás	
	deh-TRAHS	
back(s) (anatomy)	**espalda(s)**	
	es-PAHL-dah(s)	
back belt	**cinturón protector lumbar**	
	seen-too-ROHN proh-tek-TOR loom-BAR	
	faja protectora lumbar	
	FAH-ha proh-tek-TOH-rah loom-BAR	
	cinturón de soporte lumbar	
	seen-too-ROHN deh soh-POR-teh loom-BAR	
backfill (fill dirt)	**tierra de relleno**	
	tee-EH-rah deh reh-YEH-noh	
backfill (to)	**rellenar**	
	reh-yeh-NAR	
backhoe(s)	**retroexcavadora(s)**	
	reh-troh-eks-kah-vah-DOH-rah(s)	
back up (to) (vehicle)	**dar marcha atrás**	
	dar MAR-cha ah-TRAHS	
	echar en reversa	
	eh-CHAR en reh-VEHR-sah	
bad	**malo**	
	MAH-loh	
bag(s)	**bolsa(s)**	
	BOL-sah(s)	

bait (to)	**cebar** seh-BAR
bait station(s)	**estación (estaciones) de cebo** es-tah-see-OHN (es-tah-see-OH-nehs) deh SEH-boh
balcony (balconies)	**balcón (balcones)** bahl-KOHN (bahl-KOH-nes)
banana(s)	**plátano(s)** PLAH-tah-noh(s)
bandage(s)	**venda(s)** VEN-dah(s)
band saw	**sierra de cinta** see-EH rah deh SEEN-tah
bank(s)	**banco(s)** BAHN-koh(s)
bar(s)	**barra(s)** BAH-rah(s)
	barreta(s) bah-REH-tah(s)
barbecue	**barbacoa** bar-bah-KOH-ah
barbecue grill(s)	**asador(es)** ah-sah-DOR-(es)
	parrilla(s) de gas pah-REE-yah(s) deh gahs
barbed wire	**alambre de púas** ah-LAHM-breh deh POO-ahs
bark (tree)	**corteza** kor-TEH-sah

bark chips	**pedazos de corteza**
	peh-DAH-sohs deh kor-TEH-sah
	corteza de pino
	kor-TEH-sah deh PEE-noh
barricade(s)	**barricada(s)**
	bah-ree-KAH-dah(s)
barrier(s)	**barrera(s)**
	bah-REH-rah(s)
base(s)	**base(s)**
	BAH-seh(s)
basement(s)	**sótano(s)**
	SOH-tah-noh(s)
base molding	**moldura de base**
	mol-DOO-rah deh BAH-seh
basic	**básico**
	BAH-see-koh
basket(s)	**cesta(s)**
	SES-tah(s)
	canasta(s)
	kah-NAHS-tah(s)
bathe (to take a bath)	**bañarse**
	bah-NYAR-seh
bathroom(s)	**baño(s)**
	BAH-nyoh(s)
bathtub(s)	**tina(s)**
	TEE-nah(s)
	bañera(s)
	bah-NYEH-rah(s)

battery (batteries)	**batería(s)** bah-teh-REE-ah(s)
	pila(s) PEE-la(s)
battery charger(s)	**cargador(es) de batería** kar-gah-DOR-(es) deh bah-teh-REE-ah
beam(s) (ceiling)	**viga(s) de techo** VEE-gah(s) deh TEH-cho
beam hanger(s)	**estribo(s) de viga** es-TREE-boh(s) deh VEE-gah
beam pocket(s)	**ranura(s) para viga** rah-NU-rah(s) PAH-rah VEE-gah
bed(s)	**cama(s)** KAH-mah(s)
bedbugs	**chinches** CHEEN-chehs
bedroom(s)	**recámara(s)** reh-KAH-mah rah(s)
bedspread(s)	**sobrecama(s)** soh-breh-KAH-mah(s)
	colcha(s) KOL-cha(s)
bee(s)	**abeja(s)** ah-BEH-ha(s)
beehive(s)	**colmena(s)** kol-MEH-nah(s)
beetle(s)	**escarabajo(s)** es-kah-rah-BAH-ho(s)
before (earlier)	**antes** AHN-tes

begin (I)	**empiezo** em-pee-EH-soh
begin (to)	**empezar** em-peh-SAR
begin (you)	**empiece** em-pee-EH-seh
behind (in back of)	**atrás de** ah-TRAHS deh
	detrás de deh-TRAHS deh
below (under)	**abajo** ah-BAH-ho
belt(s) (clothing)	**cinturón (cinturones)** seen-too-ROHN (seen-too-ROH-nes)
belt(s) (machine)	**correa(s)** koh-REH-ah(s)
	banda(s) BAHN-dah(s)
belt(s) (sanding)	**banda(s) de lijado** BAHN-dah(s) deh lee-HA-doh
belt sander(s)	**lijadora(s) de banda** lee-ha-DOH-rah(s) deh BAHN-dah
bench(es)	**banco(s)** BAHN-koh(s)
bend (to)	**doblar** doh-BLAR
beneficial insect(s)	**insecto(s) benéfico(s)** een-SEK-toh(s) beh-NEH-fee-koh(s)
best	**mejor** meh-HOR

better	**mejor**
	meh-HOR
bicycle(s)	**bicicleta(s)**
	bee-see-KLEH-tah(s)
big	**grande**
	GRAHN-deh
bigger	**mas grande**
	mahs GRAHN-deh
biggest	**el mas grande**
	el mahs GRAHN-deh
bird(s)	**pájaro(s)**
	PAH-ha-roh(s)
bit(s) (tool)	**broca(s)**
	BROH-kah(s)
black	**negro**
	NEH-groh
blacktop	**asfalto**
	ahs-FAHL-toh
blade(s)	**hoja(s)**
	OH-ha(s)
blade(s)	**cuchilla(s)**
	koo-CHEE-yah(s)
blade(s) (saw)	**disco(s)**
	DEES-koh(s)
	hoja(s) de sierra
	OH-ha(s) deh see-EH-rah
blanket(s)	**cobija(s)**
	koh-BEE-ha(s)

bleach	**blanqueador** blahn-keh-ah-DOR
	cloro KLOH-roh
bleach (to)	**blanquear** blahn-keh-AR
block(s)	**bloque(s)** BLOH-keh(s)
blocking (carpentry)	**refuerzo** reh-FWEHR-soh
blouse(s)	**blusa(s)** BLOO-sah(s)
blow dryer(s)	**secadora(s) de pelo** seh-kah-DOH-rah(s) deh PEH-loh
blower(s)	**soplador(es)** soh-plah-DOR-(es)
blowtorch(es)	**soplete(s)** soh-PLEH-teh(s)
blue	**azul** ah-SOOL
blueprint(s)	**plano(s)** PLAH-noh(s)
board(s) (plank)	**tabla(s)** TAH-blah(s)
	tablón (tablones) tah-BLOHN (tah-BLOH-nes)
bolt(s) (hardware)	**perno(s)** PEHR-noh(s)
bolt (to fasten with a bolt)	**sujetar con perno** su-heh-TAR kohn PEHR-noh

bonus (extra pay)	**pago extraordinario** PAH-goh eks-trah-or-dee-NAH-ree-oh
book(s)	**libro(s)** LEE-broh(s)
bookcase(s)	**librero(s)** lee-BREH-roh(s)
	estantería(s) para libros es-tahn-teh-REE-ah(s) PAH-rah LEE-brohs
bookshelf (-shelves)	**estante(s) de libros** es-TAHN-teh(s) deh LEE-brohs
boot(s)	**bota(s)** BOH-tah(s)
border(s) (edge)	**borde(s)** BOR-deh(s)
border patrol	**Patrulla Fronteriza** pah-TROO-yah frohn-teh-REE-sah
	la migra lah MEE-grah
boss(es)	**jefe(s)** HEH-teh(s)
	patrón (patrones) pah-TROHN (pah-TROH-nes)
both	**los dos** lohs dohs
	ambos AHM-bohs
bottle(s)	**botella(s)** boh-TEH-yah(s)
bottom(s)	**fondo(s)** FOHN-doh(s)

bowl(s)	**plato(s) hondo(s)** PLAH-toh(s) OHN-doh(s)
	tazón grande (tazones grandes) tah-SOHN GRAHN-deh (tah-SOH-nes GRAHN-des)
box(es)	**caja(s)** KAH-ha(s)
boy(s)	**muchacho(s)** moo-CHA-cho(s)
	chico(s) CHEE-koh(s)
boyfriend(s)	**novio(s)** NOH-vee-oh(s)
brace(s) (reinforcement)	**refuerzo(s)** reh-FWEHR-soh(s)
brace (to reinforce)	**apuntalar** ah-poon-tah-LAR
	reforzar reh-for-SAR
bracing (reinforcing)	**apuntalamiento** ah-poon-tah-lah-mee-EN-toh
	reforzamiento reh-for-sah-mee-EN-toh
	arriostramiento ar-ree-oh-strah-mee-EN-toh
bracket(s)	**abrazadera(s)** ah-brah-sah-DEH-rah(s)
	soporte(s) soh-POR-teh(s)
brake(s)	**freno(s)** FREH-noh(s)

branch(es)	**rama(s)**
	RAH-mah(s)
brass	**latón**
	lah-TOHN
break(s) (brief rest)	**descanso(s)**
	des-KAHN-soh(s)
break (to damage)	**romper**
	rohm-PEHR
	quebrar
	keh-BRAR
breakfast	**desayuno**
	deh-sah-YOO-noh
brick(s)	**ladrillo(s)**
	lah-DREE-yoh(s)
	tabique(s)
	tah-BEE-keh(s)
bridge(s)	**puente(s)**
	PWEN-teh(s)
bring (I)	**traigo**
	TRI-goh
bring (to)	**traer**
	trah-EHR
bring (you)	**traiga**
	TRI-gah
broken	**roto**
	ROH-toh
	quebrado
	keh-BRAH-doh
	descompuesto
	des-kohm-PWES-toh

bronze	**bronce** BROHN-seh
broom(s)	**escoba(s)** es-KOH-bah(s)
brother(s)	**hermano(s)** ehr-MAH-noh(s)
brown	**café** kah-FEH
	marrón mah-ROHN
brush (dense growth of bushes)	**maleza** mah-LEH-sah
brush(es)	**cepillo(s)** seh-PEE-yoh(s)
brush(es) (paint)	**brocha(s)** BROH-cha(s)
brush (to)	**cepillar** seh-pee-YAR
bucket(s)	**cubeta(s)** koo-BEH-tah(s)
	balde(s) BAHL-deh(s)
bud(s)	**botón (botones)** boh-TOHN (boh-TOH-nes)
	brote(s) BROH-teh(s)
bud (to)	**brotar** broh-TAR

bug(s)	**bicho(s)** BEE-cho(s)
	insecto(s) een-SEK-toh(s)
build (I)	**construyo** kohn-STROO-yoh
build (to)	**construir** kohn-stroo-EER
build (you)	**construya** kohn-STROO-yah
builder(s)	**constructor(es)** kohn-strook-TOR-(es)
building(s)	**edificio(s)** eh-dee-FEE-see-oh(s)
building code(s)	**código(s) de construcción** KOH-dee-goh(s) deh kohn-strook-see-OHN
building permit(s)	**permiso(s) de construcción** pehr-MEE-soh(s) deh kohn-strook-see OHN
bulb(s) (flower)	**bulbo(s)** BOOL-boh(s)
bulb(s) (light)	**foco(s)** FOH-koh(s)
	bombilla(s) bohm-BEE-yah(s)
bulldozer(s)	**buldózer(es)** bool-DOH-sehr-(es)
	tractor(es) de orugas trahk-TOR-(es) deh oh-ROO-gahs
bull float(s)	**aplanadora(s) mecánica(s)** ah-plah-nah-DOH-rah(s) meh-KAH-nee-kah(s)

bungee cord(s)	**cuerda(s) elástica(s)** KWEHR-dah(s) eh-LAHS-tee-kah(s)
burn (to)	**quemar** keh-MAR
burner(s)	**mechero(s)** meh-CHEH-roh(s)
	quemador(es) keh-mah-DOR-(es)
bus(es)	**autobús (autobuses)** ow-toh-BOOS (ow-toh-BOO-ses)
bush(es)	**arbusto(s)** ar-BOOS-toh(s)
butterfly (butterflies)	**mariposa(s)** mah-ree-POH-sah(s)
button(s)	**botón (botones)** boh-TOHN (boh-TOH-nes)
buy (I)	**compro** KOHM-proh
buy (to)	**comprar** kohm-PRAR
buy (you)	**compre** KOHM-preh
cabinet(s)	**gabinete(s)** gah-bee-NEH-teh(s)
cable(s)	**cable(s)** KAH-bleh(s)
can (I)	**puedo** PWEH-doh
can (you)	**puede** PWEH-deh

can(s) (container)	**lata(s)** LAH-tah(s)
	bote(s) BOH-teh(s)
candle(s)	**vela(s)** VEH-lah(s)
can't (I)	**no puedo** noh PWEH-doh
can't (you)	**no puede** noh PWEH-deh
cap(s) (covers)	**tapa(s)** TAH-pah(s)
car(s)	**carro(s)** KAH-roh(s)
	coche(s) KOH-cheh(s)
	automóvil(es) ow-toh-MOH-veel (es)
cardboard	**cartón** kar-TOHN
cardboard box(es)	**caja(s) de cartón** KAH-ha(s) deh kar-TOHN
careful	**cuidado** kwee-DAH-doh
carefully	**cuidadosamente** kwee-dah-doh-sah-MEN-teh
carpenter(s)	**carpintero(s)** kar-peen-TEH-roh(s)
carpenter's square	**escuadra** es-KWAH-drah

carpentry	**carpintería** kar-peen-teh-REE-ah
carpet(s)	**alfombra(s)** ahl-FOHM-brah(s)
cart(s)	**carreta(s)** kah-REH-tah(s)
cartridge(s)	**cartucho(s)** kar-TOO-cho(s)
carwash	**lavacoches** lah-vah-KOH-chehs
cash	**efectivo** eh-fek-TEE-voh
casing(s) (door)	**marco(s) de puerta** MAR-koh(s) deh PWEHR-tah
casing(s) (window)	**marco(s) de ventana** MAR-koh(s) deh ven-TAH-nah
caterpillar(s)	**oruga(s)** oh-ROO-gah(s)
caulk	**sellador** seh-yah-DOR
	masilla mah-SEE-yah
	calafateo kah-lah-fah-TEH-oh
caulk (to)	**sellar** seh-YAR
	enmasillar en-mah-see-YAR
	calafatear kah-lah-fah-teh-AR

caulk gun(s)	**pistola(s) selladora(s)**	pees-TOH-lah(s) seh-yah-DOH-rah(s)
	pistola(s) de calafateo	pees-TOH-lah(s) deh kah-lah-fah-TEH-oh
caution sign(s) (safety/warning signs)	**aviso(s) de precaución**	ah-VEE-soh(s) deh pre-kow-see-OHN
	letrero(s) de precaución	leh-TREH-roh(s) deh pre-kow-see-OHN
caution tape	**cinta de advertencia**	SEEN-tah deh odd-vehr-TEN-see-ah
cave-in	**derrumbe**	dch-ROOM-beh
ceiling(s)	**techo(s)**	TEH-cho(s)
ceiling beam(s)	**viga(s) de tooho**	VEE-gah(s) deh TEH-cho
ceiling fan(s)	**ventilador(es) de techo**	ven-tee-lah-DOR-(es) deh TEH-cho
cellar(s)	**sótano(s)**	SOH-tah-noh(s)
cement	**cemento**	seh-MEN-toh
cement (glue)	**pegamento**	peh-gah-MEN-toh
cement (to)	**cementar**	seh-men-TAHR
cement truck	**camión mezcladora**	kah-mee-OHN mehs-klah-DOH-rah
center	**centro**	SEN-troh

center (to)	**centrar** sen-TRAR
cent(s)	**centavo(s)** sen-TAH-vohs
ceramic(s)	**cerámica(s)** seh-RAH-mee-kah(s)
certificate(s)	**certificado(s)** sehr-tee-fee-KAH-doh(s)
certificate of insurance	**certificado de seguro** sehr-tee-fee-KAH-doh deh seh-GOO-roh
certified	**certificado** sehr-tee-fee-KAH-doh
chain(s)	**cadena(s)** kah-DEH-nah(s)
chain saw(s)	**sierra(s) de cadena** see-EH-rah(s) deh kah-DEH-nah
	motosierra(s) moh-toh-see-EH-rah(s)
chair(s)	**silla(s)** SEE-yah(s)
chalk	**gis** hees
	tiza TEE-sah
chalk line(s)	**línea(s) de tiza** LEE-neh-ah(s) deh TEE-sah
change (to)	**cambiar** kahm-bee-AR
channel(s)	**canal(es)** kah-NAHL-(es)

charge (to) (a price/fee)	**cobrar** koh-BRAR
charger(s)	**cargador(es)** kar-gah-DOR-(es)
cheap	**barato** bah-RAH-toh
check(s) (bank)	**cheque(s)** CHEH-keh(s)
check (to)	**comprobar** kohm-proh-BAR
	verificar veh-ree-fee-KAR
cheese cloth	**estopilla** es-toh-PEE-yah
	manta de cielo MAHN-tah deh see-EH-loh
chef(s)	**cocinera(s)** koh-see-NEH-rah(s)
	cocinero(s) koh-see-NEH-roh(s)
chemical(s)	**producto(s) químico(s)** proh-DOOK-toh(s) KEE-mee-koh(s)
	sustancia(s) química(s) soos-TAHN-see-ah(s) KEE-mee-kah(s)
chemical resistant clothing	**ropa resistente a producto químico** ROH-pah reh-sees-TEN-teh ah proh-DOOK-toh KEE-mee-koh
cherry (cherries)	**cereza(s)** seh-REH-sah(s)

chicken wire	**alambre de pollo**
	ah-LAHM-breh deh POH-yoh
child(ren)	**niño(s)**
	NEE-nyoh(s)
child care	**cuidado de niños**
	kwee-DAH-doh deh NEE-nyohs
chimney(s)	**chimenea(s)**
	chee-meh-NEH-ah(s)
chisel(s)	**cincel(es)**
	seen-SEL-(es)
	formón (formones)
	for-MOHN (for-MOH-nes)
chisel (to)	**cincelar**
	seen-seh-LAR
chlorine	**cloro**
	KLOH-roh
choke(s) (engine)	**estrangulador(es)**
	es-trahn-goo-lah-DOR-(es)
choose (to)	**escoger**
	es-koh-HEHR
chop (to)	**picar**
	pee-KAR
	cortar
	kor-TAR
chop down (to)	**talar**
	tah-LAR
chop saw	**sierra de corte**
	see-EH-rah deh KOR-teh
circle(s)	**círculo(s)**
	SEER-koo-loh(s)

circuit breaker(s)	**interruptor(es) de circuito** een-teh-roop-TOR-(es) deh seer-KWEE-toh
	interruptor(es) disyuntor(es) een-teh-roop-TOR-(es) dees-yoon-TOR-(es)
circular saw	**sierra circular** see-EH-rah seer-koo-LAR
circumference(s)	**circunferencia(s)** seer-koon-feh-REN-see-ah(s)
city (cities)	**ciudad(es)** see-oo-DAHD-(es)
clamp(s)	**abrazadera(s)** ah-brah-sah-DEH-rah(s)
	mordaza(s) mor-DAH-sah(s)
	pinza(s) PEEN-sah(s)
clamp (to)	**sujetar con abrazaderas** su-heh-TAR kohn ah-brah-sah-DEH-rahs
	sujetar con pinzas su-heh-TAR kohn PEEN-sahs
clay	**arcilla** ar-SEE-yah
clean	**limpio** LEEM-pee-oh
clean (to)	**limpiar** leem-pee-AR
cleaner(s) (product)	**producto(s) de limpieza** proh-DOOK-toh(s) deh leem-pee-EH-sah
	limpiador(es) leem-pee-ah-DOR-(es)

clean this up (you)	**limpie esto**
	LEEM-pee-eh ES-toh
clear the land (to)	**despejar el terreno**
	des-peh-HAR el teh-REH-noh
	limpiar el terreno
	leem-pee-AR el teh-REH-noh
clear the land (you)	**despeje el terreno**
	des-PEH-heh el teh-REH-noh
	limpie el terreno
	LEEM-pee-eh el teh-REH-noh
clear the table (to)	**recoger la mesa**
	reh-koh-HEHR lah MEH-sah
clear the table (you)	**recoja la mesa**
	reh-KOH-ha lah MEH-sah
climb (to)	**subir**
	soo-BEER
	escalar
	es-kah-LAR
	trepar
	treh-PAR
climb (you)	**suba**
	SU-bah
	escale
	es-KAH-leh
	trepe
	TREH-peh
climbing equipment	**equipo para trepar**
	eh-KEE-poh PAH-rah treh-PAR
climbing plant	**trepadora**
	treh-pah-DOH-rah

clippers (shears)	**tijeras** tee-HEH-rahs
close (to shut)	**cerrar** seh-RAR
closed (shut)	**cerrado** seh-RAH-doh
closet(s)	**closet(s)** kloh-SEHT(S)
	ropero(s) roh-PEH-roh(s)
clothes	**ropa** ROH-pah
clothes hanger(s)	**gancho(s) para ropa** GAHN-cho(s) PAH-rah ROH-pah
clothes line(s)	**tendedero(s)** ten-deh-DEH-roh(s)
clothespin(s)	**pinza(s) para colgar la ropa** PEEN-sah(s) PAH-rah kol-GAR lah ROH-pah
clutch (vehicle)	**embrague** em-BRAH-geh
coat(s) (of paint etc.)	**capa(s)** KAH-pah(s)
cobwebs	**telarañas** teh-lah-RAH-nyahs
cockroach(es)	**cucaracha(s)** koo-kah-RAH-cha(s)
coffee	**café** kah-FEH
coffee grinder(s)	**molinillo(s) de café** moh-lee-NEE-yoh(s) deh kah-FEH

coffeemaker(s) (coffeepot)	**cafetera(s)** kah-feh-TEH-rah(s)
cold	**frío** FREE-oh
collapse (cave-in)	**derrumbe** deh-ROOM-beh
collar(s) (shirt)	**cuello(s)** KWEH-yoh(s)
color(s)	**color(es)** koh-LOR-(es)
column(s)	**columna(s)** koh-LOOM-nah(s)
come (I)	**vengo** VEN-goh
come (to)	**venir** veh-NEER
come (you)	**venga** VEN-gah
Come here!	**¡Venga aquí!** VEN-gah ah-KEE
	¡Venga acá! VEN-gah ah-KAH
community center(s)	**centro(s) social(es)** SEN-troh(s) soh-see-AHL-(es)
compact (to)	**compactar** kohm-pahk-TAR
compactor(s)	**compactador(es)** kohm-pahk-tah-DOR-(es)
company (companies)	**compañía(s)** kohm-pah-NYEE-ah(s)

| complete (to) | completar |
| | kohm-pleh-TAR |

| compost | abono orgánico |
| | ah-BOH-noh or-GAH-nee-koh |

| compressor(s) | compresor(es) |
| | kohm-preh-SOR-(es) |

| computer(s) | computadora(s) |
| | kohm-poo-tah-DOH-rah(s) |

concrete	concreto
	kohn-KREH-toh
	hormigón
	or-mee-GOHN

| concrete float(s) | llana(s) |
| | YAH-nah(s) |

concrete form(s)	cimbra(s)
	SEEM-brah(s)
	encofrado(s)
	en-koh-FRAH-doh(s)

| concrete mixer(s) | mezcladora(s) de concreto |
| | mehs-klah-DOH-rah(s) deh kohn-KREH-toh |

concrete, post-tensioned	concreto postensado
	kohn-KREH-toh pohs-ten-SAH-doh
	hormigón postensado
	or-mee-GOHN pohs-ten-SAH-doh

concrete, prestressed	concreto pretensado
	kohn-KREH-toh preh-ten-SAH-doh
	hormigón pretensado
	or-mee-GOHN preh-ten-SAH-doh

| concrete pump | equipo de bombeo de concreto |
| | eh-KEE-poh deh bohm-BEH-oh deh kohn-KREH-toh |

concrete saw	**sierra para concreto** see-EH-rah PAH-rah kohn-KREH-toh
concrete slab(s)	**losa(s) de concreto** LOH-sah(s) deh kohn-KREH-toh
concrete truck	**camión mezcladora** kah-mee-OHN mehs-klah-DOH-rah
concrete vibrator(s)	**vibrador(es) para concreto** vee-brah-DOR-(es) PAH-rah kohn-KREH-toh
conduit	**conducto** kohn-DOOK-toh
connect (to)	**conectar** koh-nek-TAR
connect (you)	**conecte** koh-NEK-teh
connection(s)	**conexión (conexiones)** koh-nek-see-OHN (koh-nek-see-OH-nes)
connector(s)	**conector(es)** koh-nek-TOR-(es)
construct (to)	**construir** kohn-stroo-EER
construction	**construcción** kohn-strook-see-OHN
construction site(s)	**sitio(s) de construcción** SEE-tee-oh(s) deh kohn-strook-see-OHN
	obra(s) de construcción OH-brah(s) deh kohn-strook-see-OHN
construction waste	**desechos de construcción** deh-SEH-chos deh kohn-strook-see-OHN
contract(s)	**contrato(s)** kohn-TRAH-toh(s)

contraction(s)	**contracción (contracciones)**
	kohn-trahk-see-OHN (kohn-trahk-see-OH-nes)
contraction joint(s)	**junta(s) de contracción**
	HOON-tah(s) deh kohn-trahk-see-OHN
contractor(s)	**contratista(s)**
	kohn-trah-TEES-tah(s)
contractor's license	**licencia de contratista**
	lee-SEN-see-ah deh kohn-trah-TEES-tah
control (to)	**controlar**
	kohn-troh-LAR
cook(s) (chef)	**cocinera(s)**
	koh-see-NEH-rah(s)
	cocinero(s)
	koh-see-NEH-roh(s)
cook (to)	**cocinar**
	koh-see-NAR
cook (you)	**cocine**
	koh SEE neh
cool (temperature)	**fresco**
	FRES-koh
cool drink	**bebida refrescante**
	beh-BEE-dah reh-fres-KAHN-teh
coolest part of the day	**horas más frescas del día**
	OH-rahs mahs FRES-kahs del DEE-ah
cool off (to refresh)	**refrescarse**
	reh-fres-KAR-seh
copper	**cobre**
	KOH-breh
cord(s)	**cordón (cordones)**
	kor-DOHN (kor-DOH-nes)

cord(s) (electrical)	**cable(s) eléctrico(s)** KAH-bleh(s) eh-LEK-tree-koh(s)
cord(s) (string)	**cuerda(s)** KWEHR-dah(s)
cordless	**inalámbrico** een-ah-LAHM-bree-koh
corner(s)	**esquina(s)** es-KEE-nah(s)
corrugated metal	**metal corrugado** meh-TAHL koh-roo-GAH-doh
	metal ondulado meh-TAHL ohn-doo-LAH-doh
couch(es)	**sofá(s)** soh-FAH(S)
count (to)	**contar** kohn-TAR
counter(s) (in a store)	**mostrador(es)** mohs-trah-DOR-(es)
countertop(s) (bathroom)	**cubierta(s) de baño** koo-bee-EHR-tah(s) deh BAH-nyoh
countertop(s) (kitchen)	**cubierta(s) de cocina** koo-bee-EHR-tah(s) deh koh-SEE-nah
cousin(s) (female)	**prima(s)** PREE-mah(s)
cousin(s) (male)	**primo(s)** PREE-moh(s)
cover(s) (lid)	**tapa(s)** TAH-pah(s)

cover (to)	**cubrir**	koo-BREER
	tapar	tah-PAR
cover (you)	**cubra**	KOO-brah
	tape	TAH-peh
crack(s) (crevice)	**grieta(s)**	gree-EH-tah(s)
	hendidura(s)	en-dee-DOO-rah(s)
crane(s) (machine)	**grúa(s)**	GROO-ah(s)
crescent wrench	**llave ajustable**	YAH-veh ah-hoos-TAH-bleh
	perico	peh-REE-koh
crew(s)	**cuadrilla(s)**	kwah-DREE-yah(s)
crib(s) (baby)	**cuna(s)**	KOO-nah(s)
crooked	**torcido**	tor-SEE-doh
cross beam(s)	**viga(s) transversal(es)**	VEE-gah(s) trans-vehr-SAHL-(es)
cross brace(s)	**refuerzo(s) transversal(es)**	reh-FWEHR-soh(s) trans-vehr-SAHL-(es)
crowbar(s)	**palanca(s)**	pah-LAHN-kah(s)

crown molding	**moldura de cornisa** mol-DOO-rah deh kor-NEE-sah
cubic foot (feet)	**pie(s) cúbico(s)** pee-eh(s) KOO-bee-koh(s)
cubic yard(s)	**yarda(s) cúbica(s)** YAR-dah(s) KOO-bee-kah(s)
cup(s)	**taza(s)** TAH-sah(s)
cupboard(s)	**trastero(s)** trahs-TEH-roh(s)
	armario(s) ar-MAH-ree-oh(s)
	aparador(es) ah-pah-rah-DOR-(es)
cup of coffee	**taza de café** TAH-sah deh kah-FEH
curb(s) (sidewalk)	**bordillo(s)** bor-DEE-yoh(s)
cure (to)	**curar** koo-RAR
cure (to) (concrete)	**fraguar** frah-GWAHR
curing	**curado** koo-RAH-doh
curing (concrete)	**fraguado** frah-GWAH-doh
curtain(s)	**cortina(s)** kor-TEE-nah(s)

cut (to)	**cortar** kor-TAR
cut (you)	**corte** KOR-teh
cutter(s)	**cortadora(s)** kor-tah-DOH-rah(s)
cutting(s) (from a plant)	**esqueje(s)** es-KEH-heh(s)
dam(s)	**presa(s)** PREH-sah(s)
	dique(s) DEE-keh(s)
	embalse(s) em-BAHL-seh(s)
dam (to)	**represar** reh-preh-SAR
	detener el agua deh-teh-NEHR el AH-gwah
damage(s)	**daño(s)** DAH-nyoh(s)
damage (to)	**dañar** dah-NYAR
damaged	**dañado** dah-NYAH-doh
damp	**húmedo** OO-meh-doh
dampen (to)	**humedecer** oo-meh-deh-SEHR
dampness	**humedad** oo-meh-DAHD

danger(s)	**peligro(s)** peh-LEE-groh(s)
dangerous	**peligroso** peh-lee-GROH-soh
darby (concrete)	**alisador de concreto** ah-lee-sah-DOR deh kohn-KREH-toh
dark	**oscuro** ohs-KOO-roh
date(s) (calendar)	**fecha(s)** FEH-cha(s)
daughter(s)	**hija(s)** EE-ha(s)
day(s)	**día(s)** DEE-ah(s)
day labor center(s)	**centro(s) de trabajo** SEN-troh(s) deh trah-BAH-ho
dead	**muerto** MWEHR-toh
debris	**basura** bah-SOO-rah
	escombros es-KOHM-brohs
	desechos deh-SEH-chos
December	**diciembre** dee-see-EM-breh
deciduous	**deciduo** deh-SEE-doo-oh
	caduco kah-DOO-koh

deck(s) (balcony)	**terraza(s)**
	teh-RAH-sah(s)
deep (depth)	**profundo**
	proh-FOON-doh
	hondo
	OHN-doh
defective	**defectuoso**
	deh-fek-too-OH-soh
defrost (to)	**descongelar**
	des-kohn-heh-LAR
defrosting	**deshielo**
	des-ee-EH-loh
deliver (to)	**entregar**
	en-treh-GAR
delivery (deliveries)	**entrega(s)**
	en-TREH-gah(s)
demolish (to)	**demoler**
	deh-moh-LEHR
	derribar
	deh-ree-BAR
demolition	**demolición**
	deh-moh-lee-see-OHN
Department of Immigration	**Departamento de Inmigración**
	deh-par-tah-MEN-toh deh een-mee-grah-see-OHN
desk(s)	**escritorio(s)**
	es-kree-TOH-ree-oh(s)
detergent(s)	**detergente(s)**
	deh-tehr-HEN-teh(s)

diagonal	**diagonal** dee-ah-goh-NAHL
diameter(s)	**diámetro(s)** dee-AH-meh-troh(s)
diaper(s)	**pañal(es)** pah-NYAHL-(es)
difficult	**difícil** dee-FEE-seel
dig (I)	**excavo** eks-KAH-voh
dig (to)	**excavar** eks-kah-VAR
dig (you)	**excave** eks-KAH-veh
digger (excavator)	**excavadora** eks-kah-vah-DOH-rah
dimension(s)	**dimensión (dimensiones)** dee-men-see-OHN (dee-men-see-OH-nes)
dining room(s)	**comedor(es)** koh-meh-DOR-(es)
dinner(s)	**cena(s)** SEH-nah(s)
dirt (filth)	**suciedad** soo-see-eh-DAHD
dirt (soil/ground)	**tierra** tee-EH-rah
dirty (filthy)	**sucio** SOO-see-oh
dirty (to make)	**ensuciar** en-soo-see-AR

disability (-ties)	**discapacidad(es)**
	dees-kah-pah-see-DAHD-(es)
	incapacidad(es)
	een-kah-pah-see-DAHD-(es)
disability insurance	**seguro de discapacidad**
	seh-GOO-roh deh dees-kah-pah-see-DAHD
	seguro de incapacidad
	seh-GOO-roh deh een-kah-pah-see-DAHD
disconnect (to)	**desconectar**
	des-koh-nek-TAR
disconnect (you)	**desconecte**
	des-koh-NEK-teh
disc sander	**lijadora de disco**
	lee-ha-DOH-rah deh DEES-koh
disease(s)	**enfermedad(es)**
	en-fehr-meh-DAHD-(es)
dish(es)	**plato(s)**
	PLAH-toh(s)
dishtowel(s)	**toalla(s) de cocina**
	toh-AH-yah(s) deh koh-SEE-nah
dishwasher	**lavaplatos**
	lah-vah-PLAH-tohs
dishwasher (machine)	**lavadora de platos**
	lah-vah-DOH-rah deh PLAH-tohs
	lavavajillas
	lah-vah-vah-HEE-yahs
disinfect (to)	**desinfectar**
	deh-seen-fek-TAR
disinfectant(s)	**desinfectante(s)**
	deh-seen-fek-TAHN-teh(s)

dismantle (to)	**desmantelar** des-mahn-teh-LAR
ditch(es) (trench)	**zanja(s)** SAHN-ha(s)
ditch digger(s) (machine)	**zanjadora(s)** sahn-ha-DOH-rah(s)
	retroexcavadora(s) reh-troh-eks-kah-vah-DOH-rah(s)
doctor(s)	**médico(s)** MEH-dee-koh(s)
dollar(s)	**dólar(es)** DOH-lar-(es)
dolly (dollies) (handcart)	**carretilla(s) de mano** kah-reh-TEE-yah(s) deh MAH-noh
	diablo(s) dee-AH-bloh(s)
door(s)	**puerta(s)** PWEHR-tah(s)
doorbell(s)	**timbre(s) para puerta** TEEM-breh(s) PAH-rah PWEHR-tah
door frame(s)	**marco(s) de puerta** MAR-koh(s) deh PWEHR-tah
door jamb(s)	**batiente(s) de la puerta** bah-tee-EN-teh(s) deh lah PWEHR-tah
	quicio(s) de la puerta KEE-see-oh(s) deh lah PWEHR-tah
doorknob(s)	**perilla(s) de puerta** peh-REE-yah(s) deh PWEHR-tah

dormant	**latente** lah-TEN-teh
	en reposo en reh-POH-soh
	inactivo ee-nahk-TEE-voh
do the dishes (to)	**lavar los platos** lah-VAR lohs PLAH-tohs
do the dishes (you)	**lave los platos** LAH-veh lohs PLAH-tohs
do the laundry (to)	**lavar la ropa** lah-VAR lah ROH-pah
do the laundry (you)	**lave la ropa** LAH-veh lah ROH-pah
double check	**doble verificación** DOH-bleh veh-ree-fee-kah-see-OHN
dowel(s)	**clavija(s)** klah-VEE-ha(s)
down (below)	**abajo** ah-BAH-ho
down here	**aquí abajo** ah-KEE ah-BAH-ho
downspout(s)	**canaleta(s)** kah-nah-LEH-tah(s)
	bajante(s) bah-HAN-teh(s)
downstairs	**abajo** ah-BAH-ho
down there	**allí abajo** ah-YEE ah-BAH-ho

drag (to)	**arrastrar**
	ah-rahs-TRAR
drag (you)	**arrastre**
	ah-RAHS-treh
drain(s)	**drenaje(s)**
	dreh-NAH-heh(s)
	desagüe(s)
	deh-SAH-gweh(s)
drain (to)	**drenar**
	dreh-NAR
drainage	**drenaje**
	dreh-NAH-heh
drainboard	**escurreplatos**
	es-koo-reh-PLAH-tohs
drainpipe(s)	**tubo(s) de drenaje**
	TOO-boh(s) deh dreh-NAH-heh
	tubo(s) de desagüe
	TOO-boh(s) deh deh-SAH-gweh
drapes (draperies)	**cortinas**
	kor-TEE-nahs
drawer(s)	**cajón (cajones)**
	kah-HOHN (kah-HOH-nes)
dress(es)	**vestido(s)**
	ves-TEE-doh(s)
dresser(s)	**cómoda(s)**
	KOH-moh-dah(s)
drill(s) (tool)	**taladro(s)**
	tah-LAH-droh(s)

drill (to)	**perforar** pehr-foh-RAR
	taladrar tah-lah-DRAR
drill bit(s)	**broca(s)** BROH-kah(s)
drill press	**prensa taladradora** PREN-sah tah-lah-drah-DOH-rah
	taladradora de columna tah-lah-drah-DOH-rah deh koh-LOOM-nah
drink(s)	**bebida(s)** beh-BEE-dah(s)
drink (to)	**tomar** toh-MAR
	beber beh-BEHR
drink (you)	**tome** TOH-meh
	beba BEH-bah
drinking fountain(s)	**bebedero(s)** beh-beh-DEH-roh(s)
drip (to)	**gotear** goh-teh-AR
drip irrigation	**riego por goteo** ree-EH-goh por goh-TEH-oh
dripping	**goteo** goh-TEH-oh
drive (to operate)	**manejar** mah-neh-HAR

driver's license	**licencia de manejo** lee-SEN-see-ah deh mah-NEH-ho
driveway(s)	**entrada(s) de auto** en-TRAH-dah(s) deh OW-toh
	entrada(s) para vehículos en-TRAH-dah(s) PAH-rah veh-EE-koo-lohs
drop (to fall)	**caer** kah-EHR
drop (to let go of)	**dejar caer** deh-HAR kah-EHR
drop ceiling	**cielo raso** see-EH-loh RAH-soh
	falso techo FAHL-soh TEH-cho
	techo colgante TEH-cho kol-GAHN-teh
drop cloth(s)	**lona(s) protectora(s)** LOH-nah(s) proh-tek-TOH-rah(s)
dry	**seco** SEH-koh
dry (to)	**secar** seh-KAR
dry (you)	**seque** SEH-keh
dry cleaners	**tintorería** teen-toh-reh-REE-ah
dry cleaning	**limpieza en seco** leem-pee-EH-sah en SEH-koh
dryer(s)	**secadora(s)** seh-kah-DOH-rah(s)

drywall	**paredes de yeso** pah-REH-des deh YEH-soh
	tablaroca tah-blah-ROH-kah
drywall mud (drywall compound)	**mezcla para paredes de yeso** MEHS-klah PAH-rah pah-REH-des deh YEH-soh
duct(s)	**conducto(s)** kohn-DOOK-toh(s)
	ducto(s) DOOK-toh(s)
dull (blunt)	**desafilado** deh-sah-fee-LAH-doh
	embotado em-boh-TAH-doh
dull (to make blunt)	**desafilar** deh-sah-fee-LAR
	embotar em-boh-TAR
dump (landfill)	**basurero** bah-su-REH-roh
	vertedero vehr-teh-DEH-roh
dump (to)	**tirar** tee-RAR
	verter vehr-TEHR
dump (you)	**tire** TEE-reh
	vierta vee-EHR-tah

dumpster(s)	**contenedor(es) de basura** kohn-teh-neh-DOR-(es) deh bah-SOO-rah
	contenedor(es) de escombros kohn-teh-neh-DOR-(es) deh es-KOHM-brohs
dump truck	**camión de volteo** kah-mee-OHN deh vol-TEH-oh
dust	**polvo** POL-voh
dust (to apply) (agriculture)	**fumigar** foo-mee-GAR
	espolvorear es-pol-voh-reh-AR
	pulverizar pool-veh-ree-SAR
dust (to dust off)	**quitar el polvo** kee-TAR el POL-voh
dust (you dust off)	**quite el polvo** KEE-teh el POL-voh
dust cloth(s)	**trapo(s) para quitar el polvo** TRAH-poh(s) PAH-rah kee-TAR el POL-voh
duster (applicator) (agriculture)	**espolvoreador** es-pol-voh-reh-ah-DOR
duster(s) (feather)	**plumero(s)** ploo-MEH-roh(s)
dust mask(s)	**mascarilla(s) contra polvo** mahs-kah-REE-yah(s) KOHN-trah POL-voh
dustpan(s)	**recogedor(es)** reh-koh-heh-DOR-(es)
dying	**muriendo** moo-ree-EN-doh

ear(s)	**oído(s)**
	oh-EE-doh(s)
earlier	**más temprano**
	MAHS tem-PRAH-noh
early	**temprano**
	tem-PRAH-noh
earmuffs (safety)	**orejeras de seguridad**
	oh-reh-HEH-rahs deh seh-goo-ree-DAHD
earn (to)	**ganar**
	gah-NAR
earplugs	**tapones para los oídos**
	tah-POH-nes PAH-rah lohs oh-EE-dohs
ear protection	**protección para la audición**
	proh-tek-see-OHN PAH-rah lah ow-dee-see-OHN
east	**este**
	ES-teh
eat (to)	**comer**
	koh-MEHR
eat (you)	**coma**
	KOH-mah
eaves	**alero**
	ah-LEH-roh
edge(s)	**orilla(s)**
	oh-REE-yah(s)
	borde(s)
	BOR-deh(s)
	filo(s)
	FEE-loh(s)
edge (to trim the edge)	**recortar la orilla**
	reh-kor-TAR lah oh-REE-yah

edger(s) (lawn)	**bordeadora(s)** bor-deh-ah-DOH-rah(s)
	orilladora(s) oh-ree-yah-DOH-rah(s)
eighth	**octavo** ohk-TAH-voh
elbow(s)	**codo(s)** KOH-doh(s)
electrical box(es)	**caja(s) eléctrica(s)** KAH-ha(s) eh-LEK-tree-kah(s)
electrical cord(s)	**cable(s) eléctrico(s)** KAH-bleh(s) eh-LEK-tree-koh(s)
electrical tape	**cinta eléctrica** SEEN-tah eh-LEK-tree-kah
electric/electical	**eléctrico** eh-LEK-tree-koh
electrician(s)	**electricista(s)** eh-lek-tree-SEES-tah(s)
electricity	**electricidad** eh-lek-tree-see-DAHD
electrocute (to)	**electrocutar** eh-lek-troh-koo-TAR
electrocution	**electrocución** eh-lek-troh-koo-see-OHN
elevation(s)	**elevación (elevaciones)** eh-leh-vah-see-OHN (eh-leh-vah-see-OH-nes)
elevator(s)	**ascensor(es)** ah-sen-SOR-(es)
	elevador(es) eh-leh-vah-DOR-(es)

email	**correo electrónico**
	koh-REH-oh eh-lek-TROH-nee-koh
emergency	**emergencia**
	eh-mehr-HEN-see-ah
emergency exit(s)	**salida(s) de emergencia**
	sah-LEE-dah(s) deh eh-mehr-HEN-see-ah
emergency shelter	**albergue de emergencia**
	ahl-BEHR-geh deh eh-mehr-HEN-see-ah
employ (to)	**emplear**
	em-pleh-AR
employee(s)	**empleado(s)**
	em-pleh-AH-doh(s)
employer(s)	**empleador(es)**
	em-pleh-ah-DOR-(es)
empty (to)	**vaciar**
	vah-see-AR
empty (unfilled)	**vacío**
	vah-SEE-oh
empty (you)	**vacíe**
	vah-SEE-eh
end (conclusion)	**fin**
	feen
end (to finish)	**terminar**
	tehr-mee-NAR
endcap(s)	**tapa(s) para extremos**
	TAH-pah(s) PAH-rah eks-TREH-mohs
engine(s)	**motor(es)**
	moh-TOR-(es)
engine(s) (two-cycle)	**motor(es) de dos tiempos**
	moh-TOR-(es) deh dohs tee-EM-pohs

English	inglés
	een-GLEHS
enough (plenty)	bastante
	bahs-TAHN-teh
	suficiente
	su-fee-see-EN-teh
entrance(s)	entrada(s)
	en-TRAH-dah(s)
equal	igual
	ee-GWAHL
equal (to make)	igualar
	ee-gwah-LAR
equipment	equipo
	eh-KEE-poh
equipment operator(s)	operador(es) de equipo
	oh-peh-rah-DOR-(es) deh eh-KEE-poh
erect scaffolding (to)	montar andamiaje
	mohn-TAR ahn-dah-mee-AH-heh
erode (to)	erosionar
	eh-roh-see-oh-NAR
erosion	erosión
	eh-roh-see-OHN
erosion control	control de la erosión
	kohn-TROL deh lah eh-roh-see-OHN
errand(s)	mandado(s)
	mahn-DAH-doh(s)
escalator(s)	escalera(s) mecánica(s)
	es-kah-LEH-rah(s) meh-KAH-nee-kah(s)

estimate(s)	**estimación (estimaciones)** es-tee-mah-see-OHN (es-tee-mah-see-OH-nes)
	cotización (cotizaciones) koh-tee-sah-see-OHN (koh-tee-sah-see-OH-nes)
estimate (to)	**estimar** es-tee-MAR
estimator(s) (person)	**evaluador(es)** eh-vahl-oo-ah-DOR-(es)
	estimador(es) es-tee-mah-DOR-(es)
even (level)	**parejo** pah-REH-ho
even (smooth surface)	**liso** LEE-soh
everyday	**todos los días** TOH-dohs lohs DEE-ahs
excavate (to)	**excavar** eks-kah-VAR
excavation(s)	**excavación (excavaciones)** eks-kah-vah-see-OHN (eks-kah-vah-see-OHN-es)
Excuse me.	**¡Discúlpeme!** dees-KOOL-peh-meh
exhaust (vehicle)	**escape** es-KAH-peh
exhaust fumes	**gas de escape** gahs deh es-KAH-peh
exhaust pipe(s)	**tubo(s) de escape** TOO-boh(s) deh es-KAH-peh

exit(s)	**salida(s)** sah-LEE-dah(s)
expansion(s)	**expansión (expansiones)** eks-pahn-see-OHN (eks-pahn-see-OH-nes)
expansion joint(s)	**junta(s) de expansión** HOON-tah(s) deh eks-pahn-see-OHN
expensive	**costoso** kohs-TOH-soh
experience(s)	**experiencia(s)** eks-peh-ree-EN-see-ah(s)
extension cord(s)	**cable(s) de extensión** KAH-bleh(s) deh eks-ten-see-OHN
	extensión(es) eléctrica(s) eks-ten-see-OHN-(es) eh-LEK-tree-kah(s)
extension ladder(s)	**escalera(s) de extensión** es-kah-LEH-rah(s) deh eks-ten-see-OHN
exterior(s)	**exterior(es)** eks-teh-ree-OR-(es)
exterminate (to)	**exterminar** eks-tehr-mee-NAR
exterminator(s)	**exterminador(es)** eks-tehr-mee-nah-DOR-(es)
eye(s)	**ojo(s)** OH-ho(s)
fabric softener	**suavizante de telas** swah-vee-SAHN-teh deh TEH-lahs
face(s)	**cara(s)** KAH-rah(s)

face shield(s)	**careta(s) facial(es)** kah-REH-tah(s) fah-see-AHL-(es)
	protector(es) para la cara proh-tek-TOR-(es) PAH-rah lah KAH-rah
fair (just)	**justo** HOOS-toh
fall (autumn)	**otoño** oh-TOH-nyoh
fall (to)	**caer** kah-EHR
fall protection	**protección contra caídas** proh-tek-see-OHN KOHN-trah kah-EE-dahs
family room(s)	**cuarto(s) de familia** KWAR-toh(s) deh fah-MEE-lee-ah
fan(s)	**abanico(s)** ah-bah-NEE-koh(s)
	ventilador(es) ven-tee-lah-DOR-(es)
fan(s) (ceiling)	**ventilador(es) de techo** ven-tee-lah-DOR-(es) deh TEH-cho
far away (distant)	**lejos** LEH-hohs
farmer(s)	**agricultor(es)** ah-gree-kool-TOR-(es)
farming	**agricultura** ah-gree-kool-TOO-rah
farm worker(s)	**trabajador(es) agrícola(s)** trah-bah-ha-DOR-(es) ah-GREE-koh-lah(s)
farther	**más lejos** mahs LEH-hohs

fascia board	**tabla frontal bajo el techo** TAH-blah frohn-TAHL BAH-ho el TEH-cho
fast	**rápido** RAH-pee-doh
fasten (to)	**fijar** fee-HAR
	sujetar su-heh-TAR
fastener(s)	**sujetador(es)** su-heh-tah-DOR-(es)
fastening (affixing)	**fijación** fee-ha-see-OHN
father(s)	**padre(s)** PAH-dreh(s)
father-in-law(s)	**suegro(s)** SWEH-groh(s)
faucet(s)	**llave(s)** YAH-veh(s)
	grifo(s) GREE-foh(s)
February	**febrero** feh-BREH-roh
feel (to touch, handle)	**tocar** toh-KAR
feet	**pies** pee-ehs
felt paper	**papel de fieltro** pah-PEL deh fee-EL-troh
fence(s)	**cerca(s)** SEHR-kah(s)

fern(s)	**helecho(s)** eh-LEH-cho(s)
fertilize (to)	**fertilizar** fehr-tee-lee-SAR
fertilizer(s)	**fertilizante(s)** fehr-tee-lee-SAHN-teh(s)
	abono(s) ah-BOH-noh(s)
fever	**flebre** fee-EH-breh
	calentura kah-len-TOO-rah
few (a)	**pocos** POH-kohs
fewer	**menos** MEH-nohs
fiberglass	**fibra de vidrio** FEE-brah deh VEE-dree-oh
field(s)	**campo(s)** KAHM-poh(s)
fifth	**quinto** KEEN-toh
fig(s)	**higo(s)** EE-goh(s)
file(s) (tool)	**lima(s)** LEE-mah(s)
file (to)	**limar** lee-MAR

fill (to)	**llenar** yeh-NAR
	rellenar reh-yeh-NAR
fill (you)	**llene** YEH-neh
filler	**relleno** reh-YEH-noh
filter(s)	**filtro(s)** FEEL-troh(s)
find (I)	**hallo** AH-yoh
	encuentro en-KWEN-troh
find (to)	**hallar** ah-YAR
	encontrar en-kohn-TRAR
find (you)	**halle** AH-yeh
	encuentre en-KWEN-treh
finger(s)	**dedo(s)** DEH-doh(s)
fingerprint(s)	**huella(s) digital(es)** WEH-yah(s) dee-hee-TAHL-(es)
finish(es) (surface coating)	**acabado(s)** ah-kah-BAH-doh(s)

finish (to)	**acabar** ah-kah-BAR
	terminar tehr-mee-NAR
finish coat	**capa de acabado** KAH-pah deh ah-kah-BAH-doh
finished?, Are you	**¿Terminó?** tehr-mee-NOH
finisher (machine)	**máquina acabadora** MAH-kee-nah ah-kah-bah-DOH-rah
finisher(s)	**acabador(es)** ah-kah-bah-DOHR-(es)
fire(s)	**fuego(s)** FWEH-goh(s)
fire escape(s)	**escalera(s) de incendios** es-kah-LEH-rah(s) deh een-SEN-dee-ohs
fire exit(s)	**salida(s) de incendios** sah-LEE-dah(s) deh een-SEN-dee-ohs
fire extinguisher(s)	**extintor(es) de incendios** eks-teen-TOR-(es) deh een-SEN-dee-ohs
	extinguidor(es) de fuegos eks-teen-gee-DOR-(es) deh FWEH-gohs
fire hazard(s)	**peligro(s) de incendio** peh-LEE-groh(s) deh een-SEN-dee-oh
fireplace(s)	**chimenea(s)** chee-meh-NEH-ah(s)
firewood	**leña** LEH-nyah
first	**primero** pree-MEH-roh

first aid	**primeros auxilios** pree-MEH-rohs ow-ZEE-lee-ohs
first aid kit	**botiquín de primeros auxilios** boh-tee-KEEN deh pree-MEH-rohs ow-ZEE-lee-ohs
fitting(s)	**conexión (conexiones)** koh-nek-see-OHN (koh-nek-see-OH-nes)
fix (to repair)	**reparar** reh-pah-RAR
	arreglar ah-reh-GLAR
	componer kohm-poh-NEHR
flagstone(s)	**losa(s) de piedra** LOH-sah(s) deh pee-EH-drah
	laja(s) LAH-ha(s)
flame(s)	**llama(s)** YAH-mah(s)
flammable	**inflamable** een-flah-MAH-bleh
flashing(s) (roof/window)	**botagua(s)** boh-TAH-gwah(s)
	tapajunta(s) tah-pah-HOON-tah(s)
flashlight(s)	**linterna(s)** leen-TEHR-nah(s)
flat (even, level)	**llano** YAH-noh
	plano PLAH-noh

flat (even surface)	**liso** LEE-soh	
flat roof	**techo plano** TEH-cho PLAH-noh	
flatten (to level)	**aplanar** ah-plah-NAR	
	nivelar nee-veh-LAR	
flat tire(s)	**llanta(s) desinflada(s)** YAHN-tah(s) deh-seen-FLAH-dah(s)	
	llanta(s) ponchada(s) YAHN-tah(s) pohn-CHA-dah(s)	
flea(s)	**pulga(s)** POOL-gah(s)	
float(s) (concrete)	**llana(s)** YAH-nah(s)	
float(s), bull	**aplanadora(s) mecánica(s)** ah-plah-nah-DOH-rah(s) meh-KAH-nee-kah(s)	
float(s), hand	**llana(s) manual(es)** YAH-nah(s) mahn-WAHL-(es)	
float (to) (concrete)	**acabar con llana** ah-kah-BAR kohn YAH-nah	
float finish (concrete)	**acabado con llana** ah-kah-BAH-doh kohn YAH-nah	
floor (ground/surface)	**suelo** SWEH-loh	
floor(s)	**piso(s)** PEE-soh(s)	
flower(s)	**flor(es)** FLOR-(es)	

flower bed(s)	**cama(s) de flores** KAH-mah(s) deh FLOR-es
flower pot(s)	**maceta(s)** mah-SEH-tah(s)
flue(s)	**escape(s) de humo** es-KAH-peh(s) deh OO-moh
fluorescent bulb(s)	**foco(s) fluorescente(s)** FOH-koh(s) floo-oh-res-SEN-teh(s)
	tubo(s) fluorescente(s) TOO-boh(s) floo-oh-res-SEN-teh(s)
fly (flies)	**mosca(s)** MOHS-kah(s)
flyswatter	**matamoscas** mah-tah-MOHS-kahs
foam	**espuma** es-POO-mah
fold (to)	**doblar** doh-BLAR
fold the clothes (you)	**doble la ropa** DOH-bleh lah ROH-pah
follow (to)	**seguir** seh-GEER
Follow me, please.	**Sígame, por favor.** SEE-gah-meh, por fah-VOR
food	**alimento** ah-lee-MEN-toh
	comida koh-MEE-dah
foot (feet)	**pie (pies)** pee-eh (pee-ehs)

footing(s) (foundation)	**cimentación (cimentaciones)** see-men-tah-see-OHN (see-men-tah-see-OH-nes)
	cimiento(s) see-mee-EN-toh(s)
footprint(s)	**huella(s)** WEH-yah(s)
fork (in road/river)	**bifurcación** bee-foor-kah-see-OHN
fork(s) (utensil)	**tenedor(es)** teh-neh-DOR-(es)
forklift	**montacargas de horquilla** mohn-tah-KAR-gahs deh or-KEE-yah
	carretilla elevadora kah-reh-TEE-yah eh-leh-vah-DOH-rah
form(s)	**forma(s)** FOR-mah(s)
form(s) (concrete)	**cimbra(s)** SEEM-brah(s)
	encofrado(s) en-koh-FRAH-doh(s)
foundation(s) (house)	**cimiento(s)** see-mee-EN-toh(s)
fountain(s)	**fuente(s)** FWEN-teh(s)
fourth	**cuarto** KWAR-toh
frame(s)	**marco(s)** MAR-koh(s)
frame (to)	**enmarcar** en-mar-KAR

frame (to) (a building)	**armar** ar-MAR	
	construir el armazón kohn-stroo-EER el ar-mah-SOHN	
framework	**armazón** ar-mah-SOHN	
	estructura es-trook-TOO-rah	
	esqueleto es-keh-LEH-toh	
framing (building)	**armazón** ar-mah-SOHN	
	entramado en-trah-MAH-doh	
	estructura es-trook-TOO-rah	
	encofrando en-koh-FRAHN-doh	
free	**libre** LEE-breh	
free (no cost)	**gratis** GRAH-tees	
freeze (to)	**congelar** kohn-heh-LAR	
freezer(s)	**congelador(es)** kohn-heh-lah-DOR-(es)	
freezing (act of)	**congelación** kohn-heh-lah-see-OHN	
freight elevator(s)	**elevador(es) de servicio** eh-leh-vah-DOR-(es) deh sehr-VEE-see-oh	

french drain(s)	**drenaje(s) tipo francés**
	dreh-NAH-heh(s) TEE-poh frahn-SEHS
	drenaje(s) cubierto con grava
	dreh-NAH-heh(s) koo-bee-EHR-toh kohn GRAH-vah
Friday	**viernes**
	vee-EHR-nes
friend(s)	**amigo(s)**
	ah-MEE-goh(s)
front(s)	**frente(s)**
	FREN-teh(s)
front end loader	**cargador frontal**
	kar-gah-DOR frohn-TAHL
frost(s)	**escarcha(s)**
	es-KAR-cha(s)
	helada(o)
	eh-LAH-dah(s)
frozen	**congelado**
	kohn-hch-LAH-doh
fruit(s)	**fruta(s)**
	FROO-tah(s)
full	**lleno**
	YEH-noh
fumes	**humos**
	OO-mohs
	vapores
	vah-POH-res
	gases
	GAH-ses
fumigate (to)	**fumigar**
	foo-mee-GAR

fumigator(s)	**fumigador(es)** foo-mee-gah-DOR-(es)
fungicide(s)	**fungicida(s)** foon-gee-SEE-dah(s)
fungus (fungi)	**hongo(s)** OHN-goh(s)
furnace(s) (heater)	**calentador(es)** kah-len-tah-DOR-(es)
furniture	**muebles** MWEH-bles
	mobiliario moh-bee-lee-AH-ree-oh
gallon(s)	**galón (galones)** gah-LOHN (gah-LOH-nes)
galvanized	**galvanizado** gahl-vah-nee-SAH-doh
garage(s)	**garaje(s)** gah-RAH-heh(s)
	cochera(s) koh-CHEH-rah(s)
garbage	**basura** bah-SOO-rah
garbage can(s)	**basurero(s)** bah-su-REH-roh(s)
	bote(s) de basura BOH-teh(s) deh bah-SOO-rah
garbage disposal(s)	**triturador(es) de basura** tree-too-rah-DOR-(es) deh bah-SOO-rah
garden(s)	**jardín (jardines)** har-DEEN (har-DEE-nes)

gardener(s)	**jardinero(s)** har-dee-NEH-roh(s)
gas	**gas** gahs
gas can(s)	**bote(s) de gasolina** BOH-teh(s) deh gah-soh-LEE-nah
gas/oil mix (for 2-cycle engine)	**mezcla de gasolina con aceite** MEHS-klah deh gah-soh-LEE-nah kohn ah-SAY-teh
gasoline	**gasolina** gah-soh-LEE-nah
gas station(s)	**gasolinera(s)** gah-soh-lee-NEH-rah(s)
gate(s)	**puerta(s) de la cerca** PWER-tah(s) deh lah SEHR-kah
	reja(s) REH-ha(s)
	portón (portones) por-TOHN (por-TOH-nes)
gear(s) (vehicle)	**marcha(s)** MAR-cha(s)
general contractor(s)	**contratista(s) general(es)** kohn-trah-TEES-tah(s) heh-neh-RAHL-(es)
generator(s)	**generador(es)** heh-neh-rah-DOR-(es)
germinate (to)	**germinar** hehr-mee-NAR
germination	**germinación** hehr-mee-nah-see-OHN
get (to fetch)	**traer** trah-EHR

get (you fetch)	**traiga** TRI-gah
get ready (to)	**preparar** preh-pah-RAR
get ready (you)	**prepare** preh-PAH-reh
girder(s)	**viga(s)** VEE-gah(s)
girl(s)	**muchacha(s)** moo-CHA-cha(s)
	chica(s) CHEE-kah(s)
girlfriend(s)	**novia(s)** NOH-vee-ah(s)
glass(es) (drinking)	**vaso(s)** VAH-soh(s)
glass (winow pane)	**vidrio** VEE-dree-oh
glasses (eye)	**lentes** LEHN-tehs
glove(s)	**guante(s)** GWAHN-teh(s)
glue(s)	**pegamento(s)** peh-gah-MEN-toh(s)
	adhesivo(s) odd-eh-SEE-voh(s)
glue (to)	**pegar** peh-GAR
glue (you)	**pegue** PEH-geh

glue gun	**pistola de pegamento**
	pees-TOH-lah deh peh-gah-MEN-toh
go forward (to)	**ir para adelante**
	eer PAH-rah ah-deh-LAHN-teh
gold	**oro**
	OH-roh
good	**bueno**
	BWEH-noh
good afternoon	**buenas tardes**
	BWEH-nahs TAR-des
good bye	**adiós**
	ah-dee-OHS
good evening	**buenas noches**
	BWEH-nahs NOH-chehs
good morning	**buenos días**
	BWEH-nohs DEE-ahs
grade (to) (land, ground)	**nivelar**
	nee-veh-LAR
	aplanar
	ah-plah-NAR
	emparejar
	em-pah-reh-HAR
	explanar
	eks-plah-NAR
grader (machine)	**máquina niveladora**
	MAH-kee-nah nee-veh-lah-DOH-rah
grading (leveling)	**nivelación**
	nee-veh-lah-see-OHN
	explanación
	eks-plah-nah-see-OHN

graft(s)	**injerto(s)** een-HEHR-toh(s)
graft (to)	**injertar** een-hehr-TAR
grandfather(s)	**abuelo(s)** ah-BWEH-loh(s)
grandmother(s)	**abuela(s)** ah-BWEH-lah(s)
grandparents	**abuelos** ah-BWEH-lohs
granite	**granito** grah-NEE-toh
grape(s)	**uva(s)** OO-vah(s)
grapefruit(s)	**toronja(s)** toh-ROHN-ha(s)
grapevine(s)	**vid(es)** VEED-(es)
	parra(s) PAH-rah(s)
grass	**pasto** PAHS-toh
	zacate sah-KAH-teh
	césped SEHS-ped
grasshopper(s)	**chapulín (chapulines)** cha-poo-LEEN (cha-poo-LEE-nes)
	saltamonte(s) sahl-tah-MOHN-teh(s)

grass seed	**semillas para césped**	
	seh-MEE-yahs PAH-rah SEHS-ped	
gravel	**grava**	
	GRAH-vah	
	cascajo	
	kahs-KAH-ho	
gray	**gris**	
	grees	
grease	**grasa**	
	GRAH-sah	
grease (to)	**engrasar**	
	cn-grah-SAR	
green	**verde**	
	VEHR-deh	
greenhouse(s)	**invernadero(s)**	
	een-vehr-nah-DEH-roh(s)	
grill (gas)	**parrilla de gas**	
	pah-REE-yah deh gahs	
grill(s) (grate)	**rejilla(s)**	
	rch-HEE-yah(s)	
grind (to)	**moler**	
	moh-LEHR	
grinder(s) (machine)	**esmeriladora(s)**	
	es-meh-ree-lah-DOH-rah(s)	
	moledora(s)	
	moh-leh-DOH-rah(s)	
groceries	**comestibles**	
	koh-mehs-TEE-blehs	
grocery store(s)	**tienda(s) de abarrotes**	
	tee-EN-dah(s) deh ah-bah-ROH-tehs	

groove(s) (slot)	**ranura(s)** rah-NU-rah(s)
ground (soil, surface)	**suelo** SWEH-loh
	tierra tee-EH-rah
grounded plug	**clavija con toma a tierra** klah-VEE-ha kohn TOH-mah ah tee-EH-rah
	clavija conectada a tierra klah-VEE-ha koh-nek-TAH-dah ah tee-EH-rah
grout	**lechada** leh-CHA-dah
grout (to)	**emboquillar** em-boh-kee-YAR
	lecharear leh-cha-reh-AR
grout float(s)	**aplicador(es) de lechada** ah-plee-kah-DOR-(es) deh leh-CHA-dah
	llana(s) de lechada YAH-nah(s) deh leh-CHA-dah
grow (to cultivate)	**cultivar** kool-tee-VAR
grower(s) (person)	**cultivador(es)** kool-tee-vah-DOR-(es)
grub(s) (insect)	**larva(s)** LAR-vah(s)
	rosquilla(s) rohs-KEE-yah(s)
	gusano(s) goo-SAH-noh(s)

guardrail(s)	**barandilla(s) de protección**
	bah-rahn-DEE-yah(s) deh proh-tek-see-OHN
	barandal(es)
	bah-rahn-DAHL-(es)
guest(s)	**huésped(es)**
	WEHS-ped-(es)
guest room(s)	**cuarto(s) de huésped**
	KWAR-toh(s) deh WEHS-ped
gutter(s) (roof)	**canaleta(s)**
	kah-nah-LEH-tah(s)
	desagüe(s)
	deh-SAH-gweh(s)
gutter(s) (street)	**canaleta(s)**
	kah-nah-LEH-tah(s)
	cuneta(s)
	koo-NEH-tah(s)
gypsum	**yeso**
	YEH-soh
hacksaw	**segueta**
	seh-GEH-tah
	sierra para metales
	see-EH-rah PAH-rah meh-TAH-lehs
hail (frozen rain)	**granizo**
	grah-NEE-soh
hail (to shower hail)	**granizar**
	grah-nee-SAR
hailstorm(s)	**granizada(s)**
	grah-nee-SAH-dah(s)
haircut(s)	**corte(s) de pelo**
	KOR-teh(s) deh PEH-loh

hair dryer(s)	**secador(es) de pelo** seh-kah-DOR-(es) deh PEH-loh	
half (halves)	**medio(s)** MEH-dee-oh(s)	
hall(s)	**vestíbulo(s)** ves-TEE-boo-loh(s)	
hallway(s)	**pasillo(s)** pah-SEE-yoh(s)	
hammer(s)	**martillo(s)** mar-TEE-yoh(s)	
hammer (to)	**clavar** klah-VAR	
hamper(s) (clothes)	**cesto(s) de ropa sucia** SES-toh(s) deh ROH-pah SOO-see-ah	
hand(s)	**mano(s)** MAH-noh(s)	
handcart(s)	**carretilla(s) de mano** kah-reh-TEE-yah(s) deh MAH-noh	
	diablo(s) dee-AH-bloh(s)	
handle(s) (knob)	**perilla(s)** peh-REE-yah(s)	
	pomo(s) POH-moh(s)	
handle(s) (tool)	**mango(s)** MAHN-goh(s)	
	asa(s) AH-sah(s)	
handrail(s)	**barandilla(s)** bah-rahn-DEE-yah(s)	

hand tool(s)	**herramienta(s) de mano**
	eh-rah-mee-EN-tah(s) deh MAH-noh
hand wash (to)	**lavar a mano**
	lah-VAR ah MAH-noh
hang (to)	**colgar**
	kol-GAR
hanger(s)	**gancho(s)**
	GAHN-cho(s)
harass (to)	**acosar**
	ah-koh-SAR
	hostigar
	ohs-tee-GAR
harassment	**acoso**
	ah-KOH-soh
	hostigamiento
	ohs-tee-gah-mee-EN-toh
hard hat(s)	**casco(s) protector(es)**
	KAHS-koh(s) proh-tek-TOR-(es)
	casco(s) duro(s)
	KAHS-koh(s) DOO-roh(s)
hardware	**herraje**
	eh-RAH-heh
hardware store	**ferretería**
	feh-reh-teh-REE-ah
harness(es) (safety)	**arnés (arneses)**
	ar-NEHS (ar-NEH-ses)
harvest (to)	**cosechar**
	koh-seh-CHAR
harvest (you)	**coseche**
	koh-SEH-cheh

hat(s)	**sombrero(s)** sohm-BREH-roh(s)
hatchet(s)	**hacha(s)** AH-cha(s)
haul (to drag)	**jalar** ha-LAR
haul (you drag)	**jale** HA-leh
hawk (mortarboard)	**tabla portamezcla** TAH-blah por-tah-MEHS-klah
hazard(s)	**peligro(s)** peh-LEE-groh(s)
hazardous	**peligroso** peh-lee-GROH-soh
hazardous chemical	**sustancia química peligrosa** soos-TAHN-see-ah KEE-mee-kah peh-lee-GROH-sah
	producto químico peligroso proh-DOOK-toh KEE-mee-koh peh-lee-GROH-soh
head(s)	**cabeza(s)** kah-BEH-sah(s)
headache(s)	**dolor(es) de cabeza** doh-LOR-(es) deh kah-BEH-sah
header(s)	**travesaño(s)** trah-veh-SAH-nyoh(s)
head protection	**protección para la cabeza** proh-tek-see-OHN PAH-rah lah kah-BEH-sah
health insurance	**seguro de salud** seh-GOO-roh deh sah-LOOD

healthy	**saludable** sah-loo-DAH-bleh
	sano SAH-noh
hear (to)	**oír** oh-EER
hearing	**oído** oh-EE-doh
heat	**calor** kah-LOR
heater(s)	**calentador(es)** kah-len-tah-DOR-(es)
heat gun	**pistola de calor** pees-TOH-lah deh kah-LOR
heating (system)	**calefacción** kah-leh-fahk-see-OHN
heavy (weight)	**pesado** peh-SAH-doh
heavy equipment	**maquinaria pesada** mah-kee-NAH-ree-ah peh-SAH-dah
hedge(s) (row of bushes)	**seto(s)** SEH-toh(s)
hedge shears	**tijeras para setos** tee-HEH-rahs PAH-rah SEH-tohs
hedge trimmers	**cortasetos** kor-tah-SEH-tohs
height (of an object)	**altura** ahl-TOO-rah
hello	**hola** OH-lah

help (I)	**ayudo** ah-YOO-doh	
help (to)	**ayudar** ah-yoo-DAR	
help (you)	**ayude** ah-YOO-deh	
Help me, please.	**Ayúdeme, por favor.** ah-YOO-deh-meh, por fah-VOR	
herbicide(s)	**herbicida(s)** ehr-bee-SEE-dah(s)	
here	**aquí** ah-KEE	
high	**alto** AHL-toh	
hinge(s)	**bisagra(s)** bee-SAH-grah(s)	
hip(s) (anatomy)	**cadera(s)** kah-DEH-rah(s)	
hip(s) (roof)	**faldón (faldones)** fahl-DOHN (fahl-DOH-nes)	
	lima tesa(s) lee-mah TEH-sah(s)	
hip board(s)	**tabla(s) para faldón** TAH-blah(s) PAH-rah fahl-DOHN	
hiring center(s)	**centro(s) de empleo** SEN-troh(s) deh em-PLEH-oh	
hit (to strike)	**pegar** peh-GAR	

hoe(s)	**azadón (azadones)** ah-sah-DOHN (ah-sah-DOH-nes)
	azada(s) ah-SAH-dah(s)
hold-down(s) (construction)	**pieza(s) de anclaje** pee-EH-sah(s) deh ahn-KLAH-heh
hole(s)	**agujero(s)** ah-goo-HEH-roh(s)
	hoyo(s) OH-yoh(s)
holiday(s)	**día(s) festivo(s)** DEE-ah(s) fes-TEE-voh(s)
	día(s) feriado(s) DEE-ah(s) feh-ree-AH-doh(s)
home(s)	**hogar(es)** oh-GAR-(es)
homeless	**sin hogar** seen oh-GAR
hook(s)	**gancho(s)** GAHN-cho(s)
hook (to)	**enganchar** en-gahn-CHAR
horizontal	**horizontal** oh-ree-sohn-TAHL
hose(s)	**manguera(s)** mahn-GEH-rah(s)
hose bibb(s)	**llave(s) de manguera** YAH-veh(s) deh mahn-GEH-rah
hose clamp(s)	**abrazadera(s) para manguera** ah-brah-sah-DEH-rah(s) PAH-rah mahn-GEH-rah

hose down (to)	**manguerear** mahn-geh-reh-AR
	regar con manguera reh-GAR kohn mahn-GEH-rah
hospital(s)	**hospital(es)** ohs-pee-TAHL-(es)
hot (temperature)	**caliente** kah-lee-EN-teh
hotel(s)	**hotel(es)** oh-TEL-(es)
hottest part of the day	**horas más caliente del día** OH-rahs mahs kah-lee-EN-teh del DEE-ah
hour(s)	**hora(s)** OH-rah(s)
house(s)	**casa(s)** KAH-sah(s)
housecleaning	**quehaceres doméstico** keh-hah-SEH-res doh-MES-tee-koh
housekeeper(s)	**ama(s) de llaves** AH-mah(s) deh YAH-vehs
	encargado(s) de limpieza en-kar-GAH-doh(s) deh leem-pee-EH-sah
housekeeping	**limpieza y mantenimiento** leem-pee-EH-sah ee mahn-teh-nee-mee-EN-toh
housework (to do)	**hacer la limpieza** ah-SEHR lah leem-pee-EH-sah
	limpiar la casa leem-pee-AR lah KAH-sah

housing development	**fraccionamiento residencial** frahk-see-ohn-ah-mee-EN-toh reh-see-den-see-AHL
	urbanización oor-bah-nee-sah-see-OHN
how	**cómo** KOH-moh
How big?	**¿Qué tan grande?** keh tahn GRAHN-deh
How far?	**¿Qué tan lejos?** keh tahn LEH-hohs
How far away?	**¿A qué distancia?** ah keh dees-TAHN-see-ah
How long? (length)	**¿Qué tan largo?** keh tahn LAR-goh
How long? (time)	**¿Cuánto tiempo?** KWAHN-toh tee-EM-poh
How many?	**¿Cuántos?** KWAHN-tohs
How much?	**¿Cuánto?** KWAHN-toh
humid	**húmedo** OO-meh-doh
humidify (to)	**humedecer** oo-meh-deh-SEHR
humidity	**humedad** oo-meh-DAHD
humus	**mantillo** mahn-TEE-yoh
hungry?, Are you	**¿Tiene hambre?** tee-EH-neh ahm-BREH

Hurry up!	**¡Apúrese!** ah-POO-reh-seh
	¡Rápido! RAH-pee-doh
hurt (to injure)	**hacer daño** ah-SEHR DAH-nyoh
	lastimar lahs-tee-MAR
husband(s)	**esposo(s)** es-POH-soh(s)
I	**yo** yoh
ice	**hielo** ee-EH-loh
ice bucket(s)	**cubeta(s) para hielo** koo-BEH-tah(s) PAH-rah ee-EH-loh
ice maker(s)	**máquina(s) para hacer hielo** MAH-kee-nah(s) PAH-rah ah-SEHR ee-EH-loh
illegal (unlawful)	**ilegal** ee-leh-GAHL
illuminate (to)	**iluminar** ee-loo-mee-NAR
illumination	**iluminación** ee-loo-mee-nah-see-OHN
immigration	**inmigración** een-mee-grah-see-OHN
in	**en** en

inch(es)	**pulgada(s)** pool-GAH-dah(s)
include (to)	**incluir** een-kloo-EER
inflammable	**inflamable** een-flah-MAH-bleh
information	**información** een-for-mah-see-OHN
inhale, don't (Don't breathe it in.)	**no respire** noh res-PEE-reh
injury (injuries) (wound)	**herida(s)** eh-REE-dah(s)
insect(s)	**insecto(s)** een-SEK-toh(s)
insecticide(s)	**insecticida(s)** een-sek-tee-SEE-dah(s)
inside	**adentro** ah-DEN-troh
	dentro DEN-troh
inspect (to)	**inspeccionar** eens-pehk-see-oh-NAR
inspection(s)	**inspección(es)** eens-pehk-see-OHN-(es)
inspector(s)	**inspector(es)** eens-pehk-TOR-(es)
install (to)	**instalar** eens-tah-LAR

installation(s)	**instalación (instalaciones)**
	eens-tah-lah-see-OHN (eens-tah-lah-see-OH-nes)
instead of	**en vez de**
	en ves deh
instruction(s)	**instrucción (instrucciones)**
	een-strook-see-OHN (een-strook-see-OH-nes)
insulate (to)	**aislar**
	ah-ees-LAR
insulating	**aislante**
	ah-ees-LAHN-teh
insulation	**aislamiento**
	ah-ees-lah-mee-EN-toh
insurance	**seguro**
	seh-GOO-roh
interior(s)	**interior(es)**
	een-teh-ree-OR-(es)
interpreter(s)	**intérprete(s)**
	een-TEHR-preh-teh(s)
iron (metal)	**hierro**
	YEH-roh
iron(s) (for clothes)	**plancha(s)**
	PLAHN-cha(s)
iron (to)	**planchar**
	plahn-CHAR
ironing board(s)	**tabla(s) de planchar**
	TAH-blah(s) deh plahn-CHAR
	burro(s)
	BOO-roh(s)
irregular	**irregular**
	ee-reh-goo-LAR

irrigate (to)	**irrigar** eer-ree-GAR
	regar reh-GAR
irrigation	**irrigación** eer-ree-gah-see-OHN
irrigation system(s)	**sistema(s) de riego** sees-TEH-mah(s) deh ree-EH-goh
ivy	**hiedra** ee-EH-drah
	enredadera en-reh-dah-DEH-rah
jack(s)	**gato(s)** GAH-toh(s)
jack(s) (hydraulic)	**gato(s) hidráulico(s)** GAH-toh(s) ee-DRAH-oo-lee-koh(s)
jacket(s)	**chamarra(s)** cha-MAH-rah(s)
	chaqueta(s) cha-KEH-tah(s)
jackhammer	**martillo hidráulico** mar-TEE-yoh ee-DRAH-oo-lee-koh
	martillo neumático mar-TEE-yoh nay-oo-MAH-tee-koh
jamb(s) (door)	**batiente(s) de la puerta** bah-tee-EN-teh(s) deh lah PWEHR-tah
	quicio(s) de la puerta KEE-see-oh(s) deh lah PWEHR-tah
janitor(s)	**empleado(s) de limpieza** em-pleh-AH-doh(s) deh leem-pee-EH-sah

janitor's closet(s)	**armario(s) del empleado de limpieza** ar-MAH-ree-oh(s) del em-pleh-AH-doh deh leem-pee-EH-sah
	closet(s) del empleado de limpieza kloh-SEHT(S) del em-pleh-AH-doh deh leem-pee-EH-sah
January	**enero** eh-NEH-roh
jet(s) (water, gas)	**chorro(s)** CHO-roh(s)
jigsaw	**sierra para contornear** see-EH-rah PAH-rah kohn-tor-neh-AR
job(s)	**trabajo(s)** trah-BAH-ho(s)
job site(s)	**lugar(es) de trabajo** loo-GAR-(es) deh trah-BAH-ho
	obra(s) OH-brah(s)
join (to connect)	**juntar** hoon-TAR
	unir oo-NEER
joint(s) (joining)	**junta(s)** HOON-tah(s)
	unión (uniones) oo-nee-OHN (oo-nee-OH-nes)
joint compound	**compuesto para juntas** kohm-PWES-toh PAH-rah HOON-tahs

jointer(s) (carpentry)	**ensambladora(s)** en-sahm-blah-DOH-rah(s)
joist(s)	**viga(s)** VEE-gah(s)
	vigueta(s) vee-GEH-tah(s)
joist hangers	**estribos para vigueta** es-TREE-bohs PAH-rah vee-GEH-tah
juice(s)	**jugo(s)** HOO-goh(s)
July	**julio** HOO-lee-oh
June	**junio** HOO-nee-oh
key(s)	**llave(s)** YAH-veh(s)
kill (to)	**matar** mah-TAR
kill (to exterminate)	**exterminar** eks-tehr-mee-NAR
kill (you)	**mate** MAH-teh
kitchen(s)	**cocina(s)** koh-SEE-nah(s)
Kleenex®	**pañuelo desechable** pahn-you-WEH-loh deh-seh-CHA-bleh
knee(s)	**rodilla(s)** roh-DEE-yah(s)
kneepads	**rodilleras** roh-dee-YEH-rahs

knife (knives)	**cuchillo(s)** koo-CHEE-yoh(s)
knob(s) (handle)	**perilla(s)** peh-REE-yah(s)
knock down (to demolish)	**tirar** tee-RAR
	derribar deh-ree-BAR
know (to)	**saber** sah-BEHR
label(s)	**etiqueta(s)** eh-tee-KEH-tah(s)
label (to)	**etiquetar** eh-tee-keh-TAR
laborer(s)	**obrero(s)** oh-BREH-roh(s)
	trabajador(es) trah-bah-ha-DOR-(es)
lacquer	**barniz** bar-NEES
	laca LAH-kah
ladder(s)	**escalera(s)** es-kah-LEH-rah(s)
ladybug(s)	**catarina(s)** kah-tah-REE-nah(s)
	mariquita(s) mah-ree-KEE-tah(s)
lamp(s)	**lámpara(s)** LAHM-pah-rah(s)

lampshade(s)	**pantalla(s)** pahn-TAH-yah(s)
land (ground)	**tierra** tee-EH-rah
land (lot, tract of land)	**terreno** teh-REH-noh
landing (stairs)	**descanso de la escalera** des-KAHN-soh deh lah es-kah-LEH-rah
landscape (the)	**jardines y áreas verdes** har-DEE-nes ee AH-reh-ahs VEHR-des
	jardinería har-dee-neh-REE-ah
landscape (to)	**hacer jardinería** ah-SEHR har-dee-neh-REE-ah
landscape lighting	**iluminación para jardín** ee-loo-mee-nah-see-OHN PAH-rah har-DEEN
landscaper(s)	**jardinero(s)** har-dee-NEH-roh(s)
landslide(s)	**derrumbe(s)** deh-ROOM-beh(s)
large	**grande** GRAHN-deh
laser level	**nivel láser** nee-VEL LAH-sehr
last (final)	**último** OOL-tee-moh
last (in the past)	**pasado** pah-SAH-doh
last week	**semana pasada** seh-MAH-nah pah-SAH-dah

late (tardy)	**tarde**	
	TAR-deh	
later (after)	**después**	
	des-PWEHS	
latex	**látex**	
	LAH-teks	
laundry (clean)	**ropa limpia**	
	ROH-pah LEEM-pee-ah	
laundry (dirty)	**ropa sucia**	
	ROH-pah SOO-see-ah	
laundry basket(s)	**cesto(s) de ropa**	
	SES-toh(s) de ROH-pah	
laundry detergent(s)	**detergente(s)**	
	deh-tehr-HEN-teh(s)	
laundry room(s)	**lavandería(s)**	
	lah-vahn-deh-REE-ah(s)	
lawn	**pasto**	
	PAHS-toh	
	zacate	
	sah-KAH-teh	
	césped	
	SEHS-ped	
lawn aerator	**aireador de césped**	
	i-reh-ah-DOR deh SEHS-ped	
lawn mower(s)	**cortadora(s) de césped**	
	kor-tah-DOH-rah(s) deh SEHS-ped	
	podadora(s) de cesped	
	poh-dah-DOH-rah(s) deh SES-ped	

lawn trimmer(s)	**orilladora(s)** oh-ree-yah-DOH-rah(s)
	podadora(s) de bordes poh-dah-DOH-rah(s) deh BOR-des
	recortadora(s) reh-kor-tah-DOH-rah(s)
lawyer(s)	**abogado(s)** ah-boh-GAH-doh(s)
layout(s)	**trazado(s)** trah-SAH-doh(s)
	trazo(s) TRAH-soh(s)
lead (metal)	**plomo** PLOH-moh
leaf (leaves)	**hoja(s)** OH-ha(s)
leaf blower(s)	**soplador(es)** soh-plah-DOR-(es)
leak(s) (in a gas/water pipe)	**fuga(s)** FOO-gah(s)
leak (to drip)	**gotear** goh-teh-AR
leaking (dripping)	**goteo** goh-TEH-oh
leather	**cuero** KWEH-roh
leave (to)	**irse** EER-seh
Leave! (you)	**¡Váyase!** VAH-yah-seh

left (side)	**izquierda** ees-kee-EHR-dah
lefthanded	**zurdo** SOOR-doh
leg(s) (animal, furniture)	**pata(s)** PAH-tah(s)
leg(s) (person, clothing)	**pierna(s)** pee-EHR-nah(s)
legal (lawful)	**legal** leh-GAHL
legal advisor(s)	**asesor(es) jurídico(s)** ah-seh-SOR-(es) hoo-REE-dee-koh(s)
lemon(s)	**limón (limones)** lee-MOHN (lee-MOH-nes)
length (measurment)	**largo** LAR-goh
length (time)	**duración** doo-rah-see-OHN
less (fewer)	**menos** MEH-nohs
lettuce	**lechuga** leh-CHOO-gah
level (flat, even)	**plano** PLAH-noh
	llano YAH-noh
level(s)	**nivel(es)** nee-VEL-(es)
level (to flatten)	**aplanar** ah-plah-NAR

level out (to)	**nivelar**	nee-veh-LAR
	explanar	eks-plah-NAR
level out (to smooth)	**allanar**	ah-yah-NAR
leveler	**nivelador**	nee-veh-lah-DOR
	niveladora	nee-veh-lah-DOH-rah
leveling	**nivelación**	nee-veh-lah-see-OHN
	explanación	eks-plah-nah-see-OHN
liability insurance	**seguro de responsabilidad civil**	seh-GOO-roh deh res-pohn-sah-bee-lee-DAHD see-VEEL
lid(s) (cover)	**tapa(s)**	TAH-pah(s)
	tapadera(s)	tah-pah-DEH-rah(s)
lift (to)	**levantar**	leh-vahn-TAR
lift (you)	**levante**	leh-VAHN-teh
light(s)	**luz (luces)**	loos (LOO-ses)
light (to ignite)	**encender**	en-sen-DEHR

light (to illuminate)	**iluminar** ee-loo-mee-NAR	
light bulb(s)	**foco(s)** FOH-koh(s)	
	bombilla(s) bohm-BEE-yah(s)	
lighting	**iluminación** ee-loo-mee-nah-see-OHN	
light switch(es)	**interruptor(es)** een-teh-roop-TOR-(es)	
like (to)	**gustar** goos-TAR	
like (you)	**gusta** GOOS-tah	
like, I	**me gusto** meh GOOS-toh	
like, I don't	**no me gusto** noh meh GOOS-toh	
limb(s) (branch)	**rama(s)** RAH-mah(s)	
lime (mineral)	**cal** kahl	
lime(s) (fruit)	**lima(s)** LEE-mah(s)	
line(s)	**línea(s)** LEE-neh-ah(s)	
linen	**ropa blanca** ROH-pah BLAHN-kah	
linen closet(s)	**armario(s) para ropa blanca** ar-MAH-ree-oh(s) PAH-rah ROH-pah BLAHN-kah	

list(s)	**lista(s)**
	LEES-tah(s)
listen (to)	**escuchar**
	es-koo-CHAR
listen (you)	**escuche**
	es-KOO-cheh
little (small)	**chico**
	CHEE-koh
living room(s)	**sala(s)**
	SAH-lah(s)
load (I)	**cargo**
	KAR-goh
load(s) (cargo/freight)	**carga(s)**
	KAR-gah(s)
load (to)	**cargar**
	kar-GAR
load (you)	**cargue**
	KAR-geh
lobby (lobbies) (entryway)	**vestíbulo(s)**
	ves-TEE-boo-loh(s)
lock(s)	**cerradura(s)**
	seh-rah-DOO-rah(s)
lock (to)	**cerrar con llave**
	seh-RAR kohn YAH-veh
lock (you)	**cierre con llave**
	see-EH-reh kohn YAH-veh
long (indicating length)	**largo**
	LAR-goh
look at (to)	**mirar**
	mee-RAR

look for (to)	**buscar** boos-KAR	
look for (you)	**busque** BOOS-keh	
Look out!	**¡Cuidado!** kwee-DAH-doh	
lubricant(s)	**lubricante(s)** loo-bree-KAHN-teh(s)	
lubricate (to)	**lubricar** loo-bree-KAR	
lumber	**madera** mah-DEH-rah	
lunch	**comida de mediodía** koh-MEE-dah deh meh-dee-oh-DEE-ah	
	almuerzo ahl-MWEHR-soh	
machine(s)	**máquina(s)** MAH-kee-nah(s)	
magazine(s)	**revista(s)** reh-VEES-tah(s)	
maggot(s)	**gusano(s)** goo-SAH-noh(s)	
maid(s)	**criada(s)** kree-AH-dah(s)	
mail	**correo** koh-REH-oh	
mail (to)	**enviar por correo** en-vee-AR por koh-REH-oh	
mailbox(es)	**buzón (buzones)** boo-SOHN (boo-SOH-nes)	

maintenance	**mantenimiento** mahn-teh-nee-mee-EN-toh
maintenance man (men)	**persona(s) de mantenimiento** pehr-SOH-nah(s) deh mahn-teh-nee-mee-EN-toh
make (to)	**hacer** ah-SEHR
make (you)	**haga** AH-gah
make the bed (to)	**hacer la cama** ah-SEHR lah KAH-mah
make the bed (you)	**haga la cama** AH-gah lah KAH-mah
mallet(s)	**mazo(s)** MAH-soh(s)
man (men)	**hombre(s)** OHM-breh(s)
manager(s)	**gerente(s)** heh-REN-teh(s)
mantelpiece(s) (fireplace)	**repisa(s) de chimenea** reh-PEE-sah(s) deh chee-meh-NEH-ah
manure	**estiércol** es-tee-EHR-kol
many	**muchos** MOO-chos
marble	**mármol** MAR-mol
March	**marzo** MAR-soh
mark(s)	**marca(s)** MAR-kah(s)

mark (to)	**marcar** mar-KAR
marker(s)	**marcador(es)** mar-kah-DOR-(es)
market(s)	**mercado(s)** mehr-KAH-doh(s)
mask(s)	**máscara(s)** MAHS-kah-rah(s)
	mascarilla(s) mahs-kah-REE-yah(s)
masking tape	**cinta adhesiva opaca** SEEN-tah odd-eh-SEE-vah oh-PAH-kah
mason(s)	**albañil(es)** ahl-bah-NYEEL-(es)
masonry	**albañilería** ahl-bah-nyee-leh-REE-ah
	mampostería mahm-pohs-teh-REE-ah
match(es) (fire)	**cerillo(s)** seh-REE-yoh(s)
match (to)	**igualar** ee-gwah-LAR
material(s)	**material(es)** mah-teh-ree-AHL-(es)
mattress(es)	**colchón (colchones)** kol-CHOHN (kol-CHOH-nes)
May	**mayo** MAH-yoh
me	**yo** yoh

| measure (to) | medir |
| | meh-DEER |

| measurement(s) | medida(s) |
| | meh-DEE-dah(s) |

measuring tape(s)	cinta(s) de medir
	SEEN-tah(s) deh meh-DEER
	cinta(s) métrica
	SEEN-tah(s) MEH-tree-kah

| mechanic(s) | mecánico(s) |
| | meh-KAH-nee-koh(s) |

| mechanical | mecánico |
| | meh-KAH-nee-koh |

| medical care | tratamiento médico |
| | trah-tah-mee-EN-toh MEH-dee-koh |

| mediterranean fruit fly | mosca mediterránea |
| | MOHS-kah meh-dee-teh-RAH-neh-ah |

| medium | mediano |
| | meh-dee-AH-noh |

| mend (to) | remendar |
| | reh-men-DAR |

| mend (you) | remiende |
| | reh-mee-EN-deh |

| mesh (wire) | malla metálica |
| | MAH-yah meh-TAH-lee-kah |

| metal(s) | metal(es) |
| | meh-TAHL-(es) |

| metallic | metálico |
| | meh-TAH-lee-koh |

| microwave oven | microondas |
| | mee-kroh-OHN-dahs |

middle	**medio** MEH-dee-oh
midnight	**medianoche** meh-dee-ah-NOH-cheh
mildew	**moho** MOH-oh
mildew (to)	**enmohecer** en-moh-eh-SEHR
mildewed	**mohoso** moh-OH-soh
mile(s)	**milla(s)** MEE-yah(s)
milk	**leche** LEH-cheh
mine (my)	**mío** MEE-oh
minimum wage	**salario mínimo** sah-LAH-ree-oh MEE-nee-moh
minute(s)	**minuto(s)** mee-NU-toh(s)
mirror(s)	**espejo(s)** es-PEH-ho(s)
miter box	**caja de ángulos** KAH-ha deh AHN-goo-lohs
	caja de ingletes KAH-ha deh een-GLEH-tes
mix (to)	**mezclar** mehs-KLAR
mix (you)	**mezcle** MEHS-kleh

mixer(s)	**mezcladora(s)** mehs-klah-DOH-rah(s)
mixture(s)	**mezcla(s)** MEHS-klah(s)
moist (damp)	**húmedo** OO-meh-doh
moisten (to dampen)	**humedecer** oo-meh-deh SEHR
moisture (dampness)	**humedad** oo-meh-DAHD
mold (mildew)	**moho** MOH-oh
mold (to become moldy)	**enmohecer** en-moh-eh-SEHR
molding (trim)	**moldura** mol-DOO-rah
moldy	**mohoso** moh-OH-soh
mole(s) (animal)	**topo(s)** TOH-poh(s)
Monday	**lunes** LOO-nes
money	**dinero** dee-NEH-roh
money order(s)	**giro(s) postal(es)** HEE-roh(s) pohs-TAHL-(es)
month(s)	**mes(es)** MEHS-(es)
mop(s)	**trapeador(es)** trah-peh-ah-DOR-(es)

mop (to)	**trapear** trah-peh-AR	
mop (you)	**trapee** trah-PEH-eh	
more	**más** mahs	
morning(s)	**mañana(s)** mah-NYAH-nah(s)	
mortar	**mezcla** MEHS-klah	
	mortero mor-TEH-roh	
mosquito(s)	**mosquito(s)** mohs-KEE-toh(s)	
moss	**musgo** MOOS-goh	
moth(s)	**palomilla(s)** pah-loh-MEE-yah(s)	
	polilla(s) poh-LEE-yah(s)	
mother(s)	**madre(s)** MAH-dreh(s)	
mother-in-law(s)	**suegra(s)** SWEH-grah(s)	
motor(s)	**motor(es)** moh-TOR-(es)	
mouse (mice)	**ratón (ratones)** rah-TOHN (rah-TOH-nes)	
mouth(s) (person)	**boca(s)** BOH-kah(s)	

move (to)	**mover** moh-VEHR
move (you)	**mueva** MWEH-vah
move/moving (to a new home)	**mudanza** moo-DAHN-sah
moving company	**compañía(s) de mudanzas** kohm-pah-NYEE-ah(s) deh moo-DAHN-sahs
mow the grass (to)	**cortar el pasto** kor-TAR el PAHS-toh
	cortar el césped kor-TAR el SEHS-ped
mow the grass (you)	**corte el pasto** KOR-teh el PAHS-toh
	corte el césped KOR-teh el SEHS-ped
much	**mucho** MOO-cho
mud	**lodo** LOH-doh
mulch	**cubierta protectora** koo-bee-EHR-tah proh-tek-TOH-rah
	material orgánico mah-teh-ree-AHL or-GAH-nee-koh
mushroom(s)	**hongo(s)** OHN-goh(s)
	seta(s) SEH-tah(s)
	champiñón (champiñones) chahm-pee-NYOHN (chahm-pee-NYOH-nes)

nail(s) (hardware)	**clavo(s)**	
	KLAH-voh(s)	
nail (to)	**clavar**	
	klah-VAR	
nail (you)	**clave**	
	KLAH-veh	
nail bag(s)	**bolsa(s) de clavos**	
	BOL-sah(s) deh KLAH-vohs	
nail driver (pneumatic)	**clavadoras neumáticas**	
	klah-vah-DOH-rahs nay-oo-MAH-tee-kahs	
nail gun(s)	**pistola(s) de clavos**	
	pees-TOH-lah(s) deh KLAH-vohs	
nail punch/set(s)	**clavador(es)**	
	klah-vah-DOR-(es)	
name(s)	**nombre(s)**	
	NOHM-breh(s)	
nap(s) (afternoon)	**siesta(s)**	
	see-ES-tah(s)	
napkin(s)	**servilleta(s)**	
	sehr-vee-YEH-tah(s)	
narrow (tight)	**estrecho**	
	es-TREH-cho	
near (close)	**cerca**	
	SEHR-kah	
near to	**cerca de**	
	SEHR-kah deh	
neat (orderly)	**ordenado**	
	or-deh-NAH-doh	
necessity (-ties)	**necesidad(es)**	
	neh-seh-see-DAHD-(es)	

neck(s)	**cuello(s)** KWEH-yoh(s)
nectarine(s)	**nectarina(s)** nek-tah-REE-nah(s)
need (I)	**necesito** neh-seh-SEE-toh
need (to)	**necesitar** neh-seh-see-TAR
need (you)	**necesite** neh-seh-SEE-teh
needle(s)	**aguja(s)** ah-GOO-ha(s)
never	**nunca** NOON-kah
new	**nuevo** NWEH-voh
newspaper(s)	**periódico(s)** peh-ree-OH-dee-koh(s)
next (afterwards)	**después** des-PWEHS
next (the following)	**próximo** PROHK-see-moh
next week	**semana próximo** seh-MAH-nah PROHK-see-moh
night(s)	**noche(s)** NOH-cheh(s)
ninth	**noveno** noh-VEH-noh

nippers (tool for nipping)	**alicates** ah-lee-KAH-tes
	tenazas teh-NAH-sahs
nitrogen	**nitrógeno** nee-TROH-heh-noh
no	**no** noh
noise(s)	**ruido(s)** roo-EE-doh(s)
noisy	**ruidoso** roo-ee-DOH-soh
noon	**mediodía** meh-dee-oh-DEE-ah
north	**norte** NOR-teh
nose(s)	**nariz (narices)** nah-REES (nah-REE-ses)
notch(es) (nick)	**muesca(s)** MWES-kah(s)
no thank you	**no gracias** noh GRAH-see-ahs
nothing	**nada** NAH-dah
November	**noviembre** noh-vee-EM-breh
now (immediately)	**ahora mismo** ah-OH-rah MEES-moh
nozzle(s)	**boquilla(s)** boh-KEE-yah(s)

number(s)	**número(s)** NU-meh-roh(s)
nursery (nurseries) (plant)	**vivero(s)** vee-VEH-roh(s)
nut(s) (edible)	**nuez (nueces)** nwes (NWEH-sehs)
nut(s) (hardware)	**tuerca(s)** TWEHR-kah(s)
October	**octubre** ohk-TOO-breh
odor(s) (smells)	**olor(es)** oh-LOR-(es)
off (to turn)	**apagar** ah-pah-GAR
off (turned)	**apagado** ah-pah-GAH-doh
office(s)	**oficina(s)** oh-fee-SEE-nah(s)
oil(s)	**aceite(s)** ah-SAY-teh(s)
oil (to)	**aceitar** ah-say-TAR
oil (two-cycle)	**aceite de motor de dos tiempos** ah-SAY-teh deh moh-TOR deh dohs tee-EM-pohs
oil change(s)	**cambio(s) de aceite** KAHM-bee-oh(s) deh ah-SAY-teh
oil filter(s)	**filtro(s) de aceite** FEEL-troh(s) deh ah-SAY-teh
okay	**está bien** es-TAH be-en

old	**viejo** vee-EH-ho
on	**a** ah
	cerca de SEHR-kah deh
	en en
	sobre SOH-breh
on (to turn)	**encender** en-sen-DEHR
on (turned)	**encendido** en-sen-DEE-doh
only	**solamente** soh-lah-MEN-teh
	único OO-nee-koh
on top of	**encima de** en-SEE-mah deh
open	**abierto** ah-bee-EHR-toh
open (to)	**abrir** ah-BREER
opening(s)	**abertura(s)** ah-behr-TOO-rah(s)
operator(s)	**operador(es)** oh-peh-rah-DOR-(es)
or	**o** oh

orange(s)	**naranja(s)**
	nah-RAHN-ha(s)
	anaranjado(s)
	ah-nah-rahn-HA-doh(s)
orchard(s)	**huerto(s)**
	WEHR-toh(s)
organic	**orgánico**
	or-GAH-nee-koh
organize (to)	**organizar**
	or-gah-nee-SAR
organize (you)	**organice**
	or-gah-NEE-seh
other	**otro**
	OH-troh
outlet(s) (electrical)	**enchufe(s) eléctrico(s)**
	en-CHOO-feh(s) eh-LEK-tree-koh(s)
	tomacorriente(s)
	toh-mah-koh-ree-EN-teh(s)
out/outside	**fuera**
	FWEH-rah
	afuera
	ah-FWEH-rah
oval(s)	**óvalo(s)**
	OH-vah-loh(s)
oven(s)	**horno(s)**
	OR-noh(s)
over	**encima de**
	en-SEE-mah deh
	sobre
	SOH-breh

overtime	**horas extras** OH-rahs EKS-trahs
overtime pay	**pago extra por horas extras** PAH-goh EKS-trah por OH-rahs EKS-trahs
overwater., Don't	**Evite regar en exceso.** eh-VEE-teh reh-GAR en eks-SEH-soh
	No aplique demasiada agua. noh ah-PLEE-keh deh-mah-see-AH-dah AH-gwah
owner(s)	**dueño(s)** DWEH-nyoh(s)
	propietario(s) proh-pee-eh-TAH-ree-oh(s)
oxidation	**oxidación** ohk-see-dah-see-OHN
oxygen	**oxígeno** ohk-SEE-heh-noh
pack (to)	**empaquetar** em-pah-keh-TAR
paint(s)	**pintura(s)** peen-TOO-rah(s)
paint (to)	**pintar** peen-TAR
paint (you)	**pinte** PEEN-teh
paintbrush(es)	**brocha(s)** BROH-cha(s)
painter(s)	**pintor(es)** peen-TOR-(es)

paint roller(s)	**rodillo(s)** roh-DEE-yoh(s)
paint sprayer(s)	**pistola(s) para pintar** pees-TOH-lah(s) PAH-rah peen-TAR
paint stripper	**removedor de pintura** reh-moh-veh-DOR deh peen-TOO-rah
paint thinner	**adelgazador de pintura** ah-del-gah-sah-DOR deh peen-TOO-rah
	disolvente para pintura dee-sol-VEN-teh PAH-rah peen-TOO-rah
palm(s)	**palma(s)** PAHL-mah(s)
palm tree(s)	**palmera(s)** pahl-MEH-rah(s)
	palma(s) PAHL-mah(s)
pan(s) (frying)	**sartén (sartenes)** sar-TEN (sar-TEH-nes)
pan(s) (saucepan)	**cacerola(s)** kah-seh-ROH-lah(s)
panel(s)	**panel(es)** pah-NEL-(es)
paneling	**paneles** pah-NEL-es
pantry (pantries)	**despensa(s)** des-PEN-sah(s)
pants (trousers)	**pantalones** pahn-tah-LOH-nes

paper(s)	**papel(es)** pah-PEL-(es)
paper towel(s)	**toalla(s) de papel** toh-AH-yah(s) deh pah-PEL
parallel	**paralelo** pah-rah-LEH-loh
park(s)	**parque(s)** PAR-keh(s)
park (to)	**estacionar** es-tah-see-oh-NAR
parking (spot/space/lot)	**estacionamiento(s)** es-tah-see-oh-nah-mee-EN-toh(s)
path(s)	**senda(s)** SEN-dah(s)
	vereda(s) veh-REH-dah(s)
patio(s)	**patio(s)** PAH-tee-oh(s)
pave (to)	**pavimentar** pah-vee-men-TAR
pavement	**pavimento** pah-vee-MEN-toh
pay (I)	**pago** PAH-goh
pay (to)	**pagar** pah-GAR
pay (you)	**pague** PAH-geh
pay attention	**preste atención** PRES-teh ah-ten-see-OHN

pay day(s)	**día(s) de pago** DEE-ah(s) deh PAH-goh
peach(es)	**durazno(s)** doo-RAHS-noh(s)
pear(s)	**pera(s)** PEH-rah(s)
peat moss	**turba** TOOR-bah
	tierra de hoja tee-EH-rah deh OH-ha
	tierra negra tee-EH-rah NEH-grah
peg(s)	**clavija(s)** klah-VEE-ha(s)
pen(s) (writing)	**pluma(s)** PLOO-mah(s)
	bolígrafo(s) boh-LEE-grah-foh(s)
pencil(s)	**lápiz (lápices)** LAH pees (LAH-pee-schs)
pepper (black)	**pimienta negra** pee-mee-EN-tah NEH-grah
pepper(s)	**pimiento(s)** pee-mee-EN-toh(s)
	chile(s) CHEE-leh(s)
perennial(s)	**perenne(s)** peh-REN-neh(s)
permit(s) (license)	**permiso(s)** pehr-MEE-soh(s)

permit(s) required	**permiso(s) requerido** pehr-MEE-soh(s) reh-keh-REE-doh
perpendicular	**perpendicular** pehr-pen-dee-koo-LAR
pest(s) (insect/animal)	**plaga(s)** PLAH-gah(s)
pest control	**control de plagas** kohn-TROL deh PLAH-gahs
pesticide(s)	**pesticida(s)** pes-tee-SEE-dah(s)
petal(s)	**pétalo(s)** PEH-tah-loh(s)
phone(s)	**teléfono(s)** teh-LEH-foh-noh(s)
phosphorous	**fósforo** FOHS-foh-roh
pick(s) (tool)	**pico(s)** PEE-koh(s)
pick (to select)	**escoger** es-koh-HEHR
pick (to harvest)	**cosechar** koh-seh-CHAR
	pizcar pees-KAR
pick (you harvest)	**coseche** koh-SEH-cheh
	pizque PEES-keh

pickax(es)	**pico(s)** PEE-koh(s)
	zapapico(s) sah-pah-PEE-koh(s)
pickup truck(s)	**camioneta(s)** kah-mee-oh-NEH-tah(s)
picture(s) (painting)	**cuadro(s)** KWAH-droh(s)
piece(s) (fragment)	**pedazo(s)** peh-DAH-soh(s)
	trozo(s) TROH-soh(s)
pile(s) (heap)	**montón (montones)** mohn-TOHN (mohn-TOH-nes)
	pila(s) PEE-lah(s)
pile (to)	**apilar** ah-pee-LAR
pillow(s)	**almohada(s)** ahl-moh-AH-dah(s)
pillowcase(s)	**funda(s) de almohada** FOON-dah(s) deh ahl-moh-AH-dah
pin(s)	**alfiler(es)** ahl-fee-LEHR (es)
pin (to)	**alfilerar** ahl-fee-leh-RAR
pine tree(s)	**pino(s)** PEE-noh(s)

pint(s)	**pinta(s)** PEEN-tah(s)
pipe(s) (tube)	**tubo(s)** TOO-boh(s)
pipe cutters	**cortatubos** kor-tah-TOO-bohs
	cortadores de tubos kor-tah-DOR-es deh TOO-bohs
pipes (plumbing)	**tubería** too-beh-REE-ah
	cañería kah-nyeh-REE-ah
pipe wrench	**llave de tubos** YAH-veh deh TOO-bohs
pit(s) (hole)	**hoyo(s)** OH-yoh(s)
	foso(s) FOH-soh(s)
pitch (roof)	**pendiente** pen-dee-EN-teh
pitch (tar)	**brea** BREH-ah
place (to)	**colocar** koh-loh-KAR
place (you)	**coloque** koh-LOH-keh
placement (positioning)	**colocación** koh-loh-kah-see-OHN
plan(s)	**plano(s)** PLAH-noh(s)

plane(s) (tool)	**cepillo(s)** seh-PEE-yoh(s)
	garlopa(s) gar-LOH-pah(s)
plane (to) (wood)	**cepillar** seh-pee-YAR
planer(s) (electrical)	**cepilladora(s) eléctrica(s)** seh-pee-yah-DOH-rah(s) eh-LEK-tree-kah(s)
plank(s)	**tabla(s)** TAH-blah(s)
	tablón (tablones) tah-BLOHN (tah-BLOH-nes)
plant(s)	**planta(s)** PLAHN-tah(s)
plant (to)	**plantar** plahn-TAR
plant (you)	**plante** PLAHN-teh
plant disease(s)	**enfermedad(es) de la planta** en-fehr-meh-DAHD-(es) deh lah PLAHN-tah
plant growth	**crecimiento de la planta** kreh-see-mee-EN-toh deh lah PLAHN-tah
plaster	**yeso** YEH-soh
plastic(s)	**plástico(s)** PLAHS-tee-koh(s)
plate(s) (construction)	**placa(s)** PLAH-kah(s)

plate(s) (dishes)	**plato(s)** PLAH-toh(s)
please	**por favor** por fah-VOR
pliers	**pinzas** PEEN-sahs
	alicates ah-lee-KAH-tehs
plug(s) (electrical)	**enchufe(s)** en-CHOO-feh(s)
	clavija(s) klah-VEE-ha(s)
plug in (to)	**enchufar** en-choo-FAR
plug up (to)	**tapar** tah-PAR
plum(s)	**ciruela(s)** seer-WEH-lah(s)
plumb (to make vertical)	**aplomar** ah-ploh-MAR
plumb (vertical)	**a plomo** ah PLOH-moh
plumber(s)	**plomero(s)** ploh-MEH-roh(s)
plumbing (pipes)	**plomería** ploh-meh-REE-ah
plumb line(s)	**plomada(s)** ploh-MAH-dah(s)
plumb rule	**nivel de perpendículo** nee-VEL deh pehr-pen-DEE-koo-loh

plunger(s) (for clogged drains)	**desatascador(es)** deh-sah-tas-kah-DOR-(es)
	destapacaños deh-stah-pah-KAH-nyohs
	destapador(es) de caños deh-stah-pah-DOR-(es) deh KAH-nyohs
plywood	**madera contrachapada** mah-DEH-rah kohn-trah-cha-PAH-dah
	triplay TREE-pli
pneumatic	**neumático** nay-oo-MAH-tee-koh
pneumatic nailer(s)	**clavadora(s) neumática(s)** klah-vah-DOH-rah(s) nay-oo-MAH-tee-kah(s)
poison(s)	**veneno(s)** veh-NEH-noh(s)
poison ivy	**hiedra venenosa** YEH-drah veh-neh-NOH-sah
poison oak	**roble venenoso** ROH-bleh veh-neh-NOH-soh
poisonous	**venenoso** veh-neh-NOH-soh
poison sumac	**zumaque venenoso** su-MAH-keh veh-neh-NOH-soh
pole(s) (stick)	**palo(s)** PAH-loh(s)
polish(es) (product)	**crema(s) para lustrar** KREH-mah(s) PAH-rah loos-TRAR
	crema(s) para pulir KREH-mah(s) PAH-rah poo-LEER

polish (to)	**lustrar** loos-TRAR
	pulir poo-LEER
polish (you)	**lustre** LOOS-treh
	pula POO-lah
polisher(s)	**máquina(s) pulidora(s)** MAH-keh-nah(s) poo-lee-DOH-rah(s)
pollen	**polen** POH-len
pollination	**polinización** poh-lee-nee-sah-see-OHN
pond(s)	**charco(s)** CHAR-koh(s)
	estanque(s) es-TAHN-keh(s)
pool(s) (swimming)	**piscina(s)** pees-SEE-nah(s)
	alberca(s) ahl-BEHR-kah(s)
portable	**portátil** por-TAH-teel
post(s) (pole)	**poste(s)** POHS-teh(s)
post hole digger	**excavadora de hoyos para postes** eks-kah-vah-DOH-rah deh OH-yohs PAH-rah POS-tehs

pot(s) (cooking)	**olla(s)** OH-yah(s)
pot(s) (flower)	**maceta(s)** mah-SEH-tah(s)
potassium	**potasio** poh-TAH-see-oh
potting soil	**tierra para macetas** tee-EH-rah PAH-rah mah-SEH-tahs
pound(s) (weight)	**libra(s)** LEE-brah(s)
power	**potencia** poh-TEN-see-ah
	poder poh-DEHR
power (energy)	**energía** eh-nehr-HEE-ah
power cord(s)	**cable(s) eléctrico(s)** KAH-bleh(s) eh-LEK-tree-koh(s)
power line(s)	**línea(s) de alto voltaje** LEE-neh-ah(s) deh AHL-toh vol-TAH-heh
power saw(s)	**sierra(s) eléctrica(s)** see-EH-rah(s) eh-LEK-tree-kah(s)
power tool(s)	**herramienta(s) eléctrica(s)** eh-rah-mee-EN-tah(s) eh-LEK-tree-kah(s)
power trowel (concrete)	**máquina extendedora de cemento** MAH-kee-nah eks-ten-deh-DOH-rah deh seh-MEN-toh
	allanadora ah-yah-nah-DOH-rah

prepare (to)	**preparar** preh-pah-RAR
prepare (you)	**prepare** preh-PAH-reh
pressure(s)	**presión (presiones)** preh-see-OHN (preh-see-OH-nes)
price(s)	**precio(s)** PREH-see-oh(s)
primer (paint)	**base de pintura** BAH-seh deh peen-TOO-rah
private	**privado** pree-VAH-doh
private property	**propiedad privada** proh-pee-eh-DAHD pree-VAH-dah
problem(s)	**problema(s)** proh-BLEH-mah(s)
project manager(s)	**gerente(s) de proyectos** heh-REN-teh(s) deh proh-YEK-tohs
propagate (to)	**propagar** proh-pah-GAR
propagation	**propagación** proh-pah-gah-see-OHN
propane gas	**gas propano** gahs proh-PAH-noh
protect (to)	**proteger** proh-teh-HEHR
protection(s)	**protección (protecciones)** proh-tek-see-OHN (proh-tek-see-OH-nes)
prune (to)	**podar** poh-DAR

prune (you)	**pode** POH-deh
pruner(s)	**podador(es)** poh-dah-DOR-(es)
pruning saw	**sierra de podar** see-EH-rah deh poh-DAR
pruning shears	**tijeras de podar** tee-HEH-rahs deh poh-DAR
pry bar(s)	**palanca(s)** pah-LAHN-kah(s)
pull (to)	**jalar** ha-LAR
pull (you)	**jale** HA-leh
pull out (to)	**arrancar** ah-rahn-KAR
pump(s)	**bomba(s)** BOHM-bah(s)
pump (to)	**bombear** bohm-beh-AR
purple	**morado** moh-RAH-doh
push (to)	**empujar** em-poo-HAR
push (you)	**empuje** em-POO-heh
put (to place)	**poner** poh-NEHR
put (you place)	**ponga** POHN-gah

put away (to)	**recoger** reh-koh-HEHR
put away (you)	**recoja** reh-KOH-ha
putty	**masilla** mah-SEE-yah
putty knife (knives)	**espátula(s)** es-PAH-too-lah(s)
quality (qualities)	**calidad(es)** kah-lee-DAHD-(es)
quantity (quantities)	**cantidad(es)** kahn-tee-DAHD-(es)
quart(s)	**cuarto(s) de galón** KWAR-toh(s) deh gah-LOHN
quarter(s) (fourths)	**cuarto(s)** KWAR-toh(s)
question(s)	**pregunta(s)** preh-GOON-tah(s)
quick	**rápido** RAH-pee-doh
	pronto PROHN-toh
quickly	**rápidamente** RAH-pee-dah-men-teh
Quiet, please.	**Silencio, por favor.** see-LEN-see-oh, por fah-VOR
rabbit(s)	**conejo(s)** koh-NEH-ho(s)
radio(s)	**radio(s)** RAH-dee-oh(s)

radius (radii)	**radio(s)** RAH-dee-oh(s)
rafter(s)	**viga(s)** VEE-gah(s)
	cabio(s) KAH-bee-oh(s)
rag(s) (cleaning)	**trapo(s)** TRAH-poh(s)
rain	**lluvia** YOO-vee-ah
raise (to hoist)	**levantar** leh-vahn-TAR
rake (roof pitch)	**inclinación** een-klee-nah-see-OHN
rake(s) (tool)	**rastrillo(s)** rahs-TREE-yoh(s)
rake (to)	**rastrillar** rahs-tree-YAR
rake (you)	**rastrille** rahs-TREE-yeh
ramp(s)	**rampa(s)** RAHM-pah(s)
range hood(s)	**campana(s) de extracción** kahm-PAH-nah(s) deh eks-trak-see-OHN
raspberry (-berries)	**frambuesa(s)** frahm-BWEH-sah(s)
rat(s)	**rata(s)** RAH-tah(s)
razor(s) (shaving)	**navaja(s) de afeitar** nah-VAH-ha(s) deh ah-fay-TAR

reach (to)	**alcanzar** ahl-kahn-SAR
reach truck	**camión de extensión** kah-mee-OHN deh eks-ten-see-OHN
	carretilla retráctil kah-reh-TEE-yah reh-TRAHK-teel
read (to)	**leer** leh-EHR
read?, Can you	**¿Sabe leer?** SAH-beh leh-EHR
rebar	**varilla** vah-REE-yah
receptacle(s)	**receptáculo(s)** reh-sep-TAH-koo-loh(s)
recipe(s)	**receta(s)** reh-SEH-tah(s)
reciprocating saw	**serrucho eléctrico** seh-ROO-cho eh-LEK-tree-koh
	sierra de vaivén see-EH-rah deh vi-VEN
rectangle(s)	**rectángulo(s)** rek-TAHN-goo-loh(s)
recycle (to)	**reciclar** reh-see-KLAR
recycling	**reciclaje** reh-see-KLAH-heh
recycling bin(s)	**receptáculo(s) de reciclaje** reh-sep-TAH-koo-loh(s) deh reh-see-KLAH-heh
red	**rojo** ROH-ho

reference(s)	**referencia(s)** reh-feh-REN-see-ah(s)
refrigeration	**refrigeración** reh-free-heh-rah-see-OHN
refrigerator(s)	**refrigerador(es)** reh-free-heh-rah-DOR-(es)
regular	**regular** reh-goo-LAR
reinforce (to)	**reforzar** reh-for-SAR
reinforcement(s)	**refuerzo(s)** reh-FWEHR-soh(s)
remember (to)	**recordar** reh-kor-DAR
remember (you)	**recuerde** reh-KWEHR-deh
remesh	**malla lisa** MAH-yah LEE-sah
remodel (to)	**remodelar** reh-moh-deh-LAR
remodeling	**remodelación** reh-moh-deh-lah-see-OHN
remote control(s)	**control(es) remoto(s)** kohn-TROL-(es) reh-MOH-toh(s)
remove (to)	**remover** reh-moh-VEHR
	quitar kee-TAR

rent (to)	**rentar** ren-TAR
	alquilar ahl-kee-LAR
repair (to)	**reparar** reh-pah-RAR
repeat (to)	**repetir** reh-peh-TEER
replace (to get another)	**reemplazar** reh-em-plah-SAR
replace (to put back)	**reponer** reh-poh-NEHR
respirator(s)	**respirador(es)** res-pee-rah-DOR-(es)
rest (to)	**descansar** des-kahn-SAR
rest (you)	**descanse** des-KAHN-seh
restroom(s)	**baño(s)** BAH-nyoh(s)
retaining wall(s)	**muro(s) de contención** MOO-roh(s) deh kohn-ten-see-OHN
	pared(es) de contención pah-RED-(es) deh kohn-ten-see-OHN
	pared(es) de retención pah-RED-(es) deh reh-ten-see-OHN
reverse gear	**marcha atrás** MAR-cha ah-TRAHS
	reversa reh-VEHR-sah

reverse (other side)	**reverso** reh-VEHR-soh
ridge(s)	**cumbre(s)** KOOM-breh(s)
ridge board(s)	**tabla(s) de cumbrera** TAH-blah(s) deh koom-BREH-rah
right (correct)	**correcto** koh-REK-toh
	bien be-en
right (side)	**derecha** deh-REH-cha
right angle(s)	**ánguio(s) recto(s)** AHN-goo-loh(s) REK-toh(s)
right here	**aquí mismo** ah-KEE MEES-moh
right there	**allí mismo** ah-YEE MEES-moh
rinse (to)	**enjuagar** en-hwah-GAR
rinse (you)	**enjuague** en-HWAH-geh
ripe (fruit)	**maduro** mah-DOO-roh
road(s)	**camino(s)** kah-MEE-noh(s)
	carretera(s) kah-reh-TEH-rah(s)

rock(s) (stones)	**piedra(s)**	
	pee-EH-drah(s)	
	roca(s)	
	ROH-kah(s)	
roller(s)	**rodillo(s)**	
	roh-DEE-yoh(s)	
roof(s)	**techo(s)**	
	TEH-cho(s)	
	techado(s)	
	teh-CHA-doh(s)	
roofer(s)	**techador(es)**	
	teh-cha-DOR-(es)	
roofing	**techado**	
	teh-CHA-doh	
roof truss(es)	**armadura(s) de cubierta**	
	ar-mah-DOO-rah(s) deh koo-bee-EHR-tah	
room(s)	**cuarto(s)**	
	KWAR-toh(s)	
room and board	**cuarto y comida**	
	KWAR-toh ee koh-MEE-dah	
root(s) (plant)	**raíz (raíces)**	
	rah-EES (rah-EE-ses)	
rope(s)	**soga(s)**	
	SOH-gah(s)	
	cuerda(s)	
	KWEHR-dah(s)	
rose(s)	**rosa(s)**	
	ROH-sah(s)	
rototiller	**aflojador de tierra**	
	ah-floh-ha-DOR deh tee-EH-rah	

round	**redondo** reh-DOHN-doh
router(s)	**fresadora(s)** freh-sah-DOH-rah(s)
	contorneadora(s) kohn-tor-neh-ah-DOH-rah(s)
router bit(s)	**broca(s)** BROH-kah(s)
rubber	**hule** OO-leh
	goma GOH-mah
	caucho KOW-cho
rug(s)	**alfombra(s)** ahl-FOHM-brah(s)
rung(s) (ladder)	**peldaño(s)** pel-DAH-nyoh(s)
runoff (excess water)	**escurrimiento** es-koo-ree-mee-EN-toh
run off (to) (excess water)	**escurrir** es-koo-REER
rust (metal)	**óxido** OHK-see-doh
	herrumbre eh-ROOM-breh
rust (plant disease)	**roya** ROH-yah
	tizón tee-SOHN

rusty (metal)	**oxidado** ohk-see-DAH-doh
	herrumbroso eh-room-BROH-soh
sack(s) (bag)	**saco(s)** SAH-koh(s)
safety	**seguridad** seh-goo-ree-DAHD
safety belt(s)	**cinturón(es) de seguridad** seen-too-ROHN-(es) deh seh-goo-ree-DAHD
safety boots	**botas de seguridad** BOH-tahs deh seh-goo-ree-DAHD
safety cone(s)	**cono(s) de seguridad** KOH-noh(s) deh seh-goo-ree-DAHD
safety earmuffs	**orejeras de seguridad** oh-reh-HEH-rahs deh seh-goo-ree-DAHD
safety equipment	**equipo de seguridad** eh-KEE-poh deh seh-goo-ree-DAHD
safety gear	**ropa de seguridad** ROH-pah deh seh-goo-ree-DAHD
safety glasses	**lentes de seguridad** LEN-tes deh seh-goo-ree-DAHD
safety goggles	**gafas de seguridad** GAH-fahs deh seh-goo-ree-DAHD
safety harness	**arnés de seguridad** ar-NEHS deh seh-goo-ree-DAHD
safety hazard(s)	**peligro(s) de seguridad** peh-LEE-groh(s) deh seh-goo-ree-DAHD

safety sign(s) (caution/warning signs)	**aviso(s) de precaución** ah-VEE-soh(s) deh pre-kow-see-OHN
	letrero(s) de precaución leh-TREH-roh(s) deh pre-kow-see-OHN
safety vest(s)	**chaleco(s) de alta visibilidad** cha-LEH-koh(s) deh AHL-tah vee-see-bee-lee-DAHD
salt	**sal** sahl
same (equal)	**igual** ee-GWAHL
sand	**arena** ah-REH-nah
sand (to)	**lijar** lee-HAR
sand (you)	**lije** LEE-heh
sandblast	**chorro de arena** CHO-roh deh ah-REH-nah
sander(s)	**lijadora(s)** lee-ha-DOH-rah(s)
sanding belt(s)	**banda(s) para lijadora** BAHN-dah(s) PAH-rah lee-ha-DOH-rah
	banda(s) de lijado BAHN-dah(s) deh lee-HA-doh
sandpaper(s)	**papel(es) de lija** pah-PEL-(es) deh LEE-ha
sandy	**arenoso** ah-reh-NOH-soh
sap (tree)	**savia** SAH-vee-ah

Saturday	**sábado** SAH-bah-doh
saucer(s)	**platillo(s)** plah-TEE-yoh(s)
saw(s)	**sierra(s)** see-EH-rah(s)
	serrucho(s) seh-ROO-cho(s)
saw(s) (hand)	**serrucho(s) de mano** seh-ROO-cho(s) deh MAH-noh
saw(s) (power)	**sierra(s) eléctrica(s)** see-EH-rah(s) eh-LEK-tree-kah(s)
saw (to)	**serruchar** seh-roo-CHAR
	cortar kor-TAR
saw (you cut)	**serruche** seh-ROO-cheh
	corte KOR-teh
saw blade(s)	**cuchilla(s)** koo-CHEE-yah(s)
	disco(s) DEES-koh(s)
	hoja(s) de sierra OH-ha(s) deh see-EH-rah
sawdust	**aserrín** ah-seh-REEN
sawhorse(s)	**caballete(s)** kah-bah-YEH-teh(s)

scaffold(s)	**andamio(s)** ahn-DAH-mee-oh(s)
scaffolding	**andamiaje** ahn-dah-mee-AH-heh
scale (insect)	**escama** es-KAH-mah
	caspilla kahs-PEE-yah
scale(s) (for weighing)	**balanza(s)** bah-LAHN-sah(s)
	báscula(s) BAHS-koo-lah(s)
school(s)	**escuela(s)** es-KWEH-lah(s)
scissors	**tijeras** tee-HEH-rahs
scrape (to)	**raspar** rahs-PAR
scraper(s)	**raspador(es)** rahs-pah-DOR-(es)
scratch (to mark)	**rayar** rah-YAR
scratch(es) (marks on a surface)	**rayado(s)** rah-YAH-doh(s)
screed (to level, make flush)	**enrasar** en-rah-SAR
screed (tool)	**enrasador** en-rah-sah-DOR
screeding (leveling, making flush)	**enrasado** en-rah-SAH-doh

screen(s) (window)	**mosquitero(s)**
	mohs-kee-TEH-roh(s)
	malla(s) de alambre
	MAH-yah(s) deh ah-LAHM-breh
	ventana(s) de tela metálica
	ven-TAH-nah(s) deh TEH-lah meh-TAH-lee-kah
screen door(s)	**puerta(s) de tela metálica**
	PWEHR-tah(s) deh TEH-lah meh-TAH-lee-kah
screw(s)	**tornillo(s)**
	tor-NEE-yoh(s)
screw (to)	**atornillar**
	ah-tor-nee-YAR
screwdriver(s)	**desarmador(es)**
	deh-sar-mah-DOR-(es)
	destornillador(es)
	des-tor-nee-yah-DOR-(es)
screwgun(s)	**atornillador(es) eléctrico(s)**
	ah-tor-nee-yah-DOR-(es) eh-LEK-tree-koh(s)
	desarmador(es) eléctrico(s)
	deh-sar-mah-DOR-(es) eh-LEK-tree-koh(s)
	destornillador(es) eléctrico(s)
	des-tor-nee-yah-DOR-(es) eh-LEK-tree-koh(s)
scrub (to)	**restregar**
	res-treh-GAR
	fregar
	freh-GAR
seal (to)	**sellar**
	seh-YAR
seal (you)	**selle**
	SEH-yeh

sealant(s)/sealer(s)	**sellador(es)** seh-yah-DOR-(es)
search for (to)	**buscar** boos-KAR
search for (you)	**busque** BOOS-keh
season(s) (of the year)	**estación (estaciones)** es-tah-see-OHN (es-tah-see-OH-nes)
seat belt(s)	**cinturón(es) de seguridad** seen-too-ROHN-(es) deh seh-goo-ree-DAHD
second(s)	**segundo(s)** seh-GOON-doh(s)
secure (to fasten)	**asegurar** ah-seh-goo-RAR
security system(s)	**sistema(s) de seguridad** sees-TEH-mah(s) deh seh-goo-ree-DAHD
see (to)	**ver** vehr
seed(s)	**semilla(s)** seh-MEE-yah(s)
seedling(s)	**plántula(s)** PLAHN-too-lah(s)
	planta(s) de semillero PLAHN-tah(s) deh seh-mee-YEH-roh
	almácigo(s) ahl-MAH-see-goh(s)
select (to)	**seleccionar** seh-lek-see-oh-NAR

selection(s)	**selección (selecciones)**
	seh-lek-see-OHN (seh-lek-see-OH-nes)
semicircle(s)	**semicírculo(s)**
	seh-mee-SEER-koo-loh(s)
send (to)	**enviar**
	en-vee-AR
separate (to)	**separar**
	seh-pah-RAR
separate (you)	**separe**
	seh-PAH-reh
September	**septiembre**
	sep-tee-EM-breh
serve (to)	**servir**
	sehr-VEER
serve food (to)	**servir la comida**
	sehr-VEER lah koh-MEE-dah
service(s)	**servicio(s)**
	sehr-VEE-see-oh(s)
service elevator(s)	**elevador(es) de servicio**
	eh-leh-vah-DOR-(es) deh sehr-VEE-see-oh
set (to put or place)	**poner**
	poh-NEHR
set the table (to)	**poner la mesa**
	poh-NEHR lah MEH-sah
set the table (you)	**ponga la mesa**
	POHN-gah lah MEH-sah
seventh	**séptimo**
	SEHP-tee-moh
sew (to)	**coser**
	koh-SEHR

sewage	**aguas negras** AH-gwahs NEH-grahs
	aguas residuales AH-gwahs reh-see-DWAH-les
sewer (pipes)	**alcantarilla** ahl-kahn-tah-REE-yah
	cloaca kloh-AH-kah
	cañería kah-nyeh-REE-ah
sewing	**costura** kohs-TOO-rah
shade (shadow)	**sombra** SOHM-brah
shaft(s) (well, mine)	**pozo(s)** POH-soh(s)
shake out (to)	**sacudir** sah-koo-DEER
shallow (depth)	**poco profundo** POH-koh proh-FOON-doh
	poco hondo POH-koh OHN-doh
shampoo(s)	**champú(s)** chahm-POO(S)
shape(s)	**forma(s)** FOR-mah(s)
	talle(s) TAH-yeh(s)

shape (to)	**formar** for-MAR
	tallar tah-YAR
sharp (sharp edged)	**filoso** fee-LOH-soh
sharpen (to)	**afilar** ah-fee-LAR
shear panels	**paneles de corte** pah-NEL-es deh KOR-teh
sheathing	**entablado** en-tah-BLAH-doh
shed(s) (storage)	**cobertizo(s)** koh-behr-TEE-soh(s)
sheet(s)	**hoja(s)** OH-ha(s)
sheet(s) (bed)	**sábana(s)** SAH-bah-nah(s)
sheet metal	**chapa metálica** CHA-pah meh-TAH-lee-kah
	lámina metálica LAH-mee-nah meh-TAH-lee-kah
	hojalata oh-ha-LAH-tah
sheet rock	**tablaroca** tah-blah-ROH-kah
shelf (shelves)	**repisa(s)** reh-PEE-sah(s)
shelving	**repisas** reh-PEE-sahs

shim(s) (wedge)	**calza(s)** KAHL-sah(s)
	cuña(s) KOO-nyah(s)
shingle(s)	**teja(s) plana(s)** TEH-ha(s) PLAH-nah(s)
	tejamanil(es) teh-ha-mah-NEEL-(es)
shirt(s)	**camisa(s)** kah-MEE-sah(s)
shoe(s)	**zapato(s)** sah-PAH-toh(s)
shopping (to go)	**ir de compras** eer deh KOHM-prahs
short (height)	**bajo** BAH-ho
short (length)	**corto** KOR-toh
shorts (clothing)	**pantalones cortos** pahn-tah-LOH-nes KOR-tohs
shoulder(s)	**hombro(s)** OHM-broh(s)
shovel(s)	**pala(s)** PAH-lah(s)
shovel (to)	**palear** pah-leh-AR
	mover con pala moh-VEHR kohn PAH-lah
show (to)	**mostrar** mohs-TRAR

shower(s)	**regadera(s)**
	reh-gah-DEH-rah(s)
	ducha(s)
	DOO-cha(s)
shower (to take a shower)	**ducharse**
	doo-CHAR-seh
shower curtain(s)	**cortina(s) de baño**
	kor-TEE-nah(s) deh BAH-nyoh
shrub(s)	**arbusto(s)**
	ar-BOOS-toh(s)
shut (to)	**cerrar**
	seh-RAR
shut (you)	**cierre**
	see-EH-reh
shutter(s) (window)	**contraventana(s)**
	kohn-trah-ven-TAH-nah(s)
	postigo(s)
	pohs-TEE-goh(s)
sick	**enfermo**
	en-FEHR-moh
sickness (disease)	**enfermedad**
	en-fehr-meh-DAHD
side(s)	**lado(s)**
	LAH-doh(s)
sidewalk(s)	**acera(s)**
	ah-SEH-rah(s)
	banqueta(s)
	bahn-KEH-tah(s)
siding	**revestimiento exterior**
	reh-ves-tee-mee-EN-toh eks-teh-ree-OR

sign(s)	**letrero(s)** leh-TREH-roh(s)
sign(s)/signal(s)	**señal(es)** seh-NYAHL-(es)
signature(s)	**firma(s)** FEER-mah(s)
Sign here.	**Firme aquí.** FEER-meh ah-KEE
silica dust	**polvo de sílice** POL-voh deh SEE-lee-seh
silver	**plata** PLAH-tah
silverware	**cubiertos** koo-bee-EHR-tohs
sink(s) (bathroom)	**lavabo(s)** lah-VAH-boh(s)
	lavamano(s) lah-vah-MAH-noh(s)
sink(s) (kitchen)	**fregadero(s)** freh-gah-DEH-roh(s)
sister(s)	**hermana(s)** ehr-MAH-nah(s)
sit (to)	**sentarse** sen-TAR-seh
Sit down, please.	**Siéntese, por favor.** see-EN-teh-seh, por fah-VOR
site(s) (job)	**sitio(s)** SEE-tee-oh(s)

sixth	**sexto** SEKS-toh	
size(s)	**tamaño(s)** tah-MAH-nyoh(s)	
size(s) (clothes)	**talla(s)** TAH-yah(s)	
skin	**piel** pee-EL	
skinny	**flaco** FLAH-koh	
skirt(s)	**falda(s)** FAHL-dah(s)	
sky	**cielo** see-EH-loh	
skylight(s)	**tragaluz (tragaluces)** trah-gah-LOOS (trah-gah-LOO-ses)	
slab(s) (concrete)	**losa(s)** LOH-sah(s)	
	piso(s) de cemento PEE-soh(s) deh seh-MEN-toh	
slate (rock)	**pizarra** pee-SAH-rah	
sledge hammer(s)	**mazo(s)** MAH-soh(s)	
sleep (to)	**dormir** dor-MEER	
sleeping	**durmiendo** dur-mee-EN-doh	

slope(s) (hillside)	**ladera(s)** lah-DEH-rah(s)
slope(s) (incline)	**pendiente(s)** pen-dee-EN-teh(s)
	inclinación (inclinaciones) een-klee-nah-see-OHN (een-klee-nah-see-OH-nes)
slow	**lento** LEN-toh
slowly	**lentamente** len-tah-MEN-teh
slug(s) (pest in garden)	**babosa(s)** bah-BOH-sah(s)
small	**pequeño** peh-KEH-nyoh
smell (to sniff)	**olfatear** ol-fah-teh-AR
smells bad (it)	**huele mal** WEH-leh mahl
smells good (it)	**huele bien** WEH-leh be-EN
smoke	**humo** OO-moh
smoke (to)	**fumar** foo-MAR
smoke alarm(s)	**alarma(s) detectora(s) de humo** ah-LAR-mah(s) deh-tek-TOH-rah(s) deh OO-moh
smooth (even, level)	**parejo** pah-REH-hoh

smooth (even surface)	**liso** LEE-soh
smooth (soft)	**suave** SWAH-veh
smooth (to)	**alisar** ah-lee-SAR
smoother	**más liso** MAHS LEE-soh
snail(s)	**caracol(es)** kah-rah-KOL-(es)
snake(s)	**víbora(s)** VEE-boh-rah(s)
	serpiente(s) sehr-pee-EN-teh(s)
snow	**nieve** nee-EH-veh
snow (to)	**nevar** neh-VAR
soak (to drench)	**empapar** em-pah-PAR
soap(s)	**jabón (jabones)** ha-BOHN (ha-BOH-nes)
soap dish(es)	**jabonera(s)** ha-boh-NEH-rah(s)
Social Security number	**número de Seguro Social** NU-meh-roh deh seh-GOO-roh soh-see-AHL
sock(s) (clothing)	**calcetín (calcetines)** kahl-seh-TEEN (kahl-seh-TEE-nes)
socket(s) (electrical)	**enchufe(s)** en-CHOO-feh(s)

socket wrench(es)	**llave(s) de tubos**
	YAH-veh(s) deh TOO-bohs
	llave(s) de cubo
	YAH-veh(s) deh KOO-boh
	llave(s) de copa
	YAH-veh(s) deh KOH-pah
sod (to)	**cubrir de césped**
	koo-BREER deh SEHS-ped
sod (turf)	**tepe**
	TEH-peh
soffit(s)	**sofito(s)**
	soh-FEE-toh(s)
	plafón (plafones)
	plah-FOHN (plah-FOH-nes)
soil	**suelo**
	SWEH-loh
	tierra
	tee-EH-rah
soil amendments	**corrección de suelos**
	koh-rek-see-OHN deh SWEH-lohs
	enmiendas de suelos
	en-mee-EN-dahs deh SWEH-lohs
solar light(s)	**luz (luces) solar**
	loos (LOO-sehs) soh-LAR
solder	**soldadura**
	sol-dah-DOO-rah
solder (to)	**soldar**
	sol-DAR
soldering gun	**pistola para soldar**
	pees-TOH-lah PAH-rah sol-DAR

| solvent(s) | solvente(s) |
| | sol-VEN-teh(s) |

| son(s) | hijo(s) |
| | EE-ho(s) |

| Sorry. (I am sorry.) | Lo siento. |
| | loh see-EN-toh |

| Sorry! (Pardon me!) | ¡Perdón! |
| | pehr-DOHN |

| south | sur |
| | soor |

spade(s) (tool)	pala(s)
	PAH-lah(s)
	laya(s)
	LAH-yah(s)

| Spanish | español |
| | es-pah-NYOL |

| spark plug(s) | bujía(s) |
| | boo-HEE-ah(s) |

| spatula(s) | espátula(s) |
| | es-PAH-too-lah(s) |

| speak (I) | hablo |
| | AH-bloh |

| speak (to) | hablar |
| | ah-BLAR |

| speak (you) | hable |
| | AH-bleh |

| spider(s) | araña(s) |
| | ah-RAH-nyah(s) |

| spider web(s) | telaraña(s) |
| | teh-lah-RAH-nyah(s) |

spill (to)	**derramar** deh-rah-MAR
splice (to)	**empalmar** em-pahl-MAR
	unir oo-NEER
sponge(s)	**esponja(s)** es-POHN-ha(s)
spoon(s)	**cuchara(s)** koo-CHA-rah(s)
spot(s) (mark/stain)	**mancha(s)** MAHN-cha(s)
spray (to)	**rociar** roh-see-AR
spray (you)	**rocíe** roh-SEE-eh
sprayer(s) (garden)	**aspersor(es)** ahs-pehr-SOR-(es)
	rociador(es) roh-see-ah-DOR-(es)
	bomba(s) para fumigar BOHM-bah(s) PAH-rah foo-mee-GAR
spray gun (paint)	**pistola para pintar** pees-TOH-lah PAH-rah peen-TAR
spray paint	**pintura en aerosol** peen-TOO-rah en i-roh-SOL
spread (I)	**distribuyo** dees-tree-BOO-yoh
	desparramo des-pah-RAH-moh

spread (to)	**distribuir**
	dees-tree-BWEER
	desparramar
	des-pah-rah-MAR
spread (you)	**distribuya**
	dees-tree-BOO-yah
	desparrame
	des-pah-RAH-meh
spreader(s) (tool)	**esparcidor(es)**
	es-par-see-DOR-(es)
spring(s) (coil)	**resorte(s)**
	reh-SOR-teh(s)
spring (season)	**primavera**
	pree-mah-VEH-rah
sprinkler(s)	**rociador(es)**
	roh-see-ah-DOR-(es)
	aspersor(es)
	ahs-pehr-SOR-(es)
	irrigador(es)
	eer-ree-gah-DOR-(es)
sprinkler system(s)	**sistema(s) de riego**
	sees-TEH-mah(s) deh ree-EH-goh
sprout (to germinate)	**brotar**
	broh-TAR
square(s) (carpenter's)	**escuadra(s)**
	es-KWAH-drah(s)
square(s) (shape)	**cuadrado(s)**
	kwah-DRAH-doh(s)
square foot (feet)	**pie(s) cuadrado(s)**
	pee-eh(s) kwah-DRAH-doh(s)

square yard(s)	**yarda(s) cuadrada(s)**
	YAR-dah(s) kwah-DRAH-dah(s)
squeegee(s)	**escurridor(es) de hule**
	es-koo-ree-DOR-(es) deh OO-leh
	limpiador(es) de goma
	leem-pee-ah-DOR-(es) deh GOH-mah
squirrel(s)	**ardilla(s)**
	ar-DEE-yah(s)
stack (to)	**apilar**
	ah-pee-LAR
stack (you)	**apile**
	ah-PEE-leh
stain(s) (dye)	**tinte(s)**
	TEEN-tch(s)
stain(s) (for wood)	**tinte(s) para madera**
	TEEN-teh(s) PAH-rah mah-DEH-rah
stain(s) (spot/mark)	**mancha(s)**
	MAHN-cha(s)
stainless steel	**acero inoxidable**
	ah-SEH-roh een-ohk-see-DAH-bleh
stair(s) (step)	**escalón (escalones)**
	es-kah-LOHN (es-kah-LOH-nes)
stairs (stairway)	**escaleras**
	es-kah-LEH-rahs
stairwell(s)	**hueco(s) de la escalera**
	WEH-koh(s) deh lah es-kah-LEH-rah
stake(s)	**estaca(s)**
	es-TAH-kah(s)
stake (to)	**estacar**
	es-tah-KAR

stake (you)	**estace** es-TAH-seh
staple(s)	**grapa(s)** GRAH-pah(s)
staple (to)	**engrapar** en-grah-PAR
staple gun(s)	**pistola(s) engrapadora(s)** pees-TOH-lah(s) en-grah-pah-DOH-rah(s)
starch (for clothes)	**almidón** ahl-mee-DOHN
starch (spray starch)	**almidón en aerosol** ahl-mee-DOHN en i-roh-SOL
starch (to)	**almidonar** ahl-mee-doh-NAR
start (to begin)	**empezar** em-peh-SAR
start (you begin)	**empiece** em-pee-EH-seh
start here (you)	**empiece aquí** em-pee-EH-seh ah-KEE
stay (to)	**quedarse** keh-DAR-seh
Stay! (you)	**¡Quédese!** KEH-deh-seh
steel	**acero** ah-SEH-roh
stem(s) (stalk)	**tallo(s)** TAH-yoh(s)

step(s) (rung)	**peldaño(s)**	
	pel-DAH-nyoh(s)	
step(s) (stair)	**escalón (escalones)**	
	es-kah-LOHN (es-kah-LOH-nes)	
stepladder(s)	**escalera(s) de tijera**	
	es-kah-LEH-rah(s) deh tee-HEH-rah	
stick (to attach)	**pegar**	
	peh-GAR	
sticker(s) (label)	**etiqueta(s)**	
	eh-tee-KEH-tah(s)	
stilts	**zancos**	
	SAHN-kohs	
stomach(s)	**estómago(s)**	
	es-TOH-mah-goh(s)	
stomachache(s)	**dolor(es) de estómago**	
	doh-LOR-(es) deh es-TOH-mah-goh	
stone(s)	**piedra(s)**	
	pee-EH-drah(s)	
stonework	**mampostería de piedra**	
	mahm-pohs-teh-REE-ah deh pee-EH-drah	
stop (halt)	**alto**	
	AHL-toh	
Stop!	**¡Deténgase!**	
	deh-TEN-gah-seh	
store(s) (shops)	**tienda(s)**	
	tee-EN-dah(s)	
store (to)	**almacenar**	
	ahl-mah-seh-NAR	

storeroom(s)	**almacén (almacenes)** ahl-mah-SEN (ahl-mah-SEH-nes)
	bodega(s) boh-DEH-gah(s)
storm(s)	**tormenta(s)** tor-MEN-tah(s)
stove(s) (cooking)	**cocina(s)** koh-SEE-nah(s)
stove(s) (heating)	**estufa(s)** es-TOO-fah(s)
straight (not bent)	**derecho** deh-REH-cho
	recto REK-toh
straight edge	**borde recto** BOR-deh REK-toh
strap(s)	**correa(s)** koh-REH-ah(s)
strawberry (-berries)	**fresa(s)** FREH-sah(s)
steam	**vapor** vah-POR
steamroller	**aplanadora** ah-plan-ah-DOR-ah
street(s)	**calle(s)** KAH-yeh(s)
stretch out (to)	**estirar** es-tee-RAR
	alargar ah-lar-GAR

string(s)	**cordón (cordones)** kor-DOHN (kor-DOH-nes)
	cuerda(s) KWEHR-dah(s)
strip the paint (to)	**quitar la pintura** kee-TAR lah peen-TOO-rah
structure(s)	**estructura(s)** es-trook-TOO-rah(s)
stucco	**estuco** es-TOO-koh
stucco (to)	**colocar estuco** koh-loh-KAR es-TOO-koh
	estucar es-too-KAR
stud(s) (beam)	**viga(s)** VEE-gah(s)
	barrote(s) bah-ROH-teh(s)
stud(s) (wall)	**montante(s)** mohn-TAHN-teh(s)
stump(s) (tree)	**cepa(s)** SEH-pah(s)
	tocón (tocones) toh-KOHN (toh-KOH-nes)
subcontractor(s)	**subcontratista(s)** soob-kohn-trah-TEES-tah(s)
sugar	**azúcar** ah-SOO-kar
suit(s) (clothing)	**traje(s)** TRAH-heh(s)

suitcase(s)	**maleta(s)** mah-LEH-tah(s)
summer	**verano** veh-RAH-noh
sun	**sol** sol
Sunday	**domingo** doh-MEEN-goh
sunlight	**luz del sol** loos del sol
supper	**cena** SEH-nah
supplies	**materiales** mah-teh-ree-AH-lehs
support(s)	**soporte(s)** soh-POR-teh(s)
	apoyo(s) ah-POH-yoh(s)
support (to)	**soportar** soh-por-TAR
	apoyar ah-poh-YAR
surface(s)	**superficie(s)** su-pehr-FEE-see-eh(s)
surveyor(s)	**agrimensor(es)** ah-gree-men-SOR-(es)
sweep (to)	**barrer** bah-REHR
sweep (you)	**barra** BAH-rah

swimming pool(s)	**alberca(s)** ahl-BEHR-kah(s)
	piscina(s) pees-SEE-nah(s)
switch(es)	**interruptor(es)** een-teh-roop-TOR-(es)
switchplate(s)	**placa(s) del interruptor** PLAH-kah(s) del een-teh-roop-TOR
system(s)	**sistema(s)** sees-TEH-mah(s)
table(s)	**mesa(s)** MEH-sah(s)
tablecloth(s)	**mantel(es)** mahn-TEL-(es)
table saw	**sierra de mesa** see-EH-rah deh MEH-sah
tack(s) (nails)	**tachuela(s)** tah-CHWEH-lah(s)
tack (to fasten)	**sujetar con tachuelas** soo-heh-TAR kohn tah-CHWEH-lahs
take (I)	**tomo** TOH-moh
take (to)	**tomar** toh-MAR
take (you)	**tome** TOH-meh
take out (to remove)	**sacar** sah-KAR
tall	**alto** AHL-toh

tamp (to)	**apisonar** ah-pee-soh-NAR
tamper(s) (tool)	**pisón (pisones)** pee-SOHN (pee-SOH-nes)
	apisonadora(s) ah-pee-soh-nah-DOH-rah(s)
tangerine(s)	**mandarina(s)** mahn-dah-REE-nah(s)
tank(s)	**tanque(s)** TAHN-keh(s)
tape(s)	**cinta(s)** SEEN-tah(s)
tape (to)	**poner cinta** poh-NEHR SEEN-tah
tape measure(s)	**cinta(s) de medir** SEEN-tah(s) deh meh-DEER
	cinta(s) métrica SEEN-tah(s) MEH-tree-kah
taping knife (knives)	**espátula(s)** es-PAH-too-lah(s)
tar	**brea** BREH-ah
	chapapote cha-pah-POH-teh
tarp(s)	**lona(s)** LOH-nah(s)
taste (flavor)	**sabor** sah-BOHR
teach (to)	**enseñar** en-seh-NYAR

teeth	**dientes** dee-EN-tehs
telephone(s)	**teléfono(s)** teh-LEH-foh-noh(s)
television(s)	**televisión (televisiones)** teh-leh-vee-see-OHN (teh-leh-vee-see-OH-nes)
temperature(s)	**temperatura(s)** tem-peh-rah-TOO-rah(s)
temporary	**temporal** tem-poh-RAHL
tenth	**déclmo** DEH-see-moh
termite(s)	**termita(s)** tehr-MEE-tah(s)
terrace(s)	**terraza(s)** teh-RAH-sah(s)
texture(s)	**textura(s)** teks-TOO-rah(s)
thank you	**gracias** GRAH-see-ahs
that	**ese** EH-seh
	aquel ah-KEL
that's all	**eso es todo** EH-soh es TOH-doh
thawing	**deshielo** des-YEH-loh
thaw (to)	**descongelar** des-kohn-heh-LAR

there	**allí**
	ah-YEE
	allá
	ah-YAH
these	**estos**
	ES-tohs
	estas
	ES-tahs
thick	**grueso**
	gru-EH-soh
thin	**delgado**
	del-GAH-doh
think (to)	**pensar**
	pen-SAR
thinner (paint)	**adelgazador**
	ah-del-gah-sah-DOR
	disolvente
	dee-sol-VEN-teh
third	**tercero**
	tehr-SEH-roh
thirsty	**sediento**
	seh-dee-EN-toh
this	**este**
	ES-teh
	esta
	ES-tah
those	**esos**
	EH-sohs
	aquellos
	ah-KEH-yohs

thread(s)	**hilo(s)** EE-loh(s)
threshold(s)	**umbral(es)** oom-BRAHL-(es)
throttle(s)	**válvula(s) reguladora(s)** VAHL-voo-lah(s) reh-goo-lah-DOH-rah(s)
throw away (to)	**tirar a la basura** tee-RAR ah la bah-SOO-rah
thumb(s)	**pulgar(es)** pool-GAR-(es)
Thursday	**jueves** HWEH-vehs
tie (to)	**atar** ah-TAR
	amarrar ah-mah-RAR
tie wire(s)	**alambre(s) de amarre** ah-LAHM-breh(s) deh ah-MAH-reh
tile(s)	**azulejo(s)** ah-su-LEH-ho(s)
	baldosa(s) bahl-DOH-sah(s)
	loseta(s) loh-SEH-tah(s)
	teja(s) TEH-ha(s)
	mosaico(s) moh-sah-EE-koh(s)

tile (to)	**azulejar**	ah-su-leh-HAR
	baldosar	bahl-doh-SAR
	tejar	teh-HAR
tiled roof	**tejado**	teh-HA-doh
time(s)	**tiempo(s)**	tee-EM-poh(s)
timer(s)	**interruptor(es) automático(s)**	een-teh-roop-TOR-(es) ow-toh-MAH-tee-koh(s)
	temporizador(es)	tem-poh-ree-sah-DOR-(es)
tin (metal)	**estaño**	es-TAH-nyoh
tint(s)	**tinta(s)**	TEEN-tah(s)
tint (to)	**tintar**	teen-TAR
tips (gratuities)	**propinas**	proh-PEE-nahs
tire(s)	**llanta(s)**	YAHN-tah(s)
tissue(s) (Klennex®)	**pañuelo(s) desechable(s)**	pahn-you-WEH-loh(s) deh-seh-CHA-bleh(s)
toaster(s)	**tostador(es)**	tohs-tah-DOR-(es)
today	**hoy**	oy

toe(s)	**dedo(s) del pie** DEH-doh(s) del pee-eh
toilet(s)	**inodoro(s)** ee-noh-DOH-roh(s)
	excusado(s) eks-koo-SAH-doh(s)
toilet brush(es)	**cepillo(s) para limpiar el excusado** seh-PEE-yoh(s) PAH-rah leem-pee-AR el eks-koo-SAH-doh
toilet paper	**papel de baño** pah-PEL deh BAH-nyoh
	papel higiénico pah-PEL ee-hee-EH-nee-koh
toilet paper holder	**portarrollos del baño** por-tah-ROH-yohs del BAH-nyoh
toilet seat(s)	**asiento(s) del excusado** ah-see-EN-toh(s) del eks-koo-SAH-doh
	asiento(s) del inodoro ah-see-EN-toh(s) del ee-noh-DOH-roh
tomato(es)	**tomate(s)** toh-MAH-teh(s)
	jitomate(s) hee-toh-MAH-teh(s)
tomorrow	**mañana** mah-NYAH-nah
ton(s)	**tonelada(s)** toh-neh-LAH-dah(s)
tongue(s)	**lengua(s)** LEN-gwah(s)

tonight	**esta noche** ES-tah NOH-cheh
tool(s)	**herramienta(s)** eh-rah-mee-EN-tah(s)
tool belt	**portaherramientas** por-tah-eh-rah-mee-EN-tahs
tool box(es)	**caja(s) de herramientas** KAH-ha(s) deh eh-rah-mee-EN-tahs
tooth (teeth)	**diente(s)** dee-EN-teh(s)
top (on top of)	**encima de** en-SEE-mah deh
top(s) (cover)	**tapa(s)** TAH-pah(s)
top (upper)	**superior** su-peh-ree-OR
top coat (finish coat)	**capa final** KAH-pah fee-NAHL
topsoil	**mantillo** mahn-TEE-yoh
	capa arable KAH-pah ah-RAH-bleh
	suelo cultivable SWEH-loh kool-tee-VAH-bleh
torch(es)	**antorcha(s)** ahn-TOR-cha(s)
torch(es) (blowtorch)	**soplete(s)** soh-PLEH-teh(s)

torque (to)	**potencia de torsión** poh-TEN-see-ah deh tor-see-OHN
	par de torsión par deh tor-see-OHN
torque wrench	**llave de torsión** YAH-veh deh tor-see-OHN
touch (to feel, handle)	**tocar** toh-KAR
tow (to)	**remolcar** reh-mol-KAR
tow (you)	**remolca** reh-MOL-kah
towel(s)	**toalla(s)** toh-AH-yah(s)
towel bar(s)	**toallero(s)** toh-ah-YEH-roh(s)
towing	**remolque** reh-MOL-keh
toy(s)	**juguete(s)** hoo-GEH-teh(s)
tractor(s)	**tractor(es)** trahk-TOR-(es)
trailer(s)	**remolque(s)** reh-MOL-keh(s)
train (to)	**entrenar** en-treh-NAR
trainer(s)	**entrenador(es)** en-treh-nah-DOR-(es)

training (job)	**enseñanza** en-seh-NYAHN-sah
	entrenamiento en-treh-nah-mee-EN-toh
transformer(s)	**transformador(es)** trahns-for-mah-DOR-(es)
transit(s) (surveying)	**teodolito(s)** teh-oh-doh-LEE-toh(s)
translator(s)	**traductor(es)** trah-dook-TOR-(es)
transplant (to)	**transplantar** trahns-plahn-TAR
trap(s)	**trampa(s)** TRAHM-pah(s)
trash	**basura** bah-SOO-rah
	descho deh-SEH-cho
trash bag(s)	**bolsa(s) para basura** BOL-sah(s) PAH-rah bah-SOO-rah
trash can(s)	**bote(s) de basura** BOH-teh(s) deh bah-SOO-rah
tray(s)	**charola(s)** cha-ROH-lah(s)
	bandeja(s) bahn-DEH-ha(s)
tread(s) (stair)	**huella(s) de escalón** WEH-yah(s) deh es-kah-LOHN
tree(s)	**árbol(es)** AR-bol-(es)

trellis(es)	**enrejado(s)** en-reh-HA-doh(s)
trench(es) (ditch)	**zanja(s)** SAHN-ha(s)
trespass (to)	**entrar ilegalmente** en-TRAHR ee-leh-gahl-MEN-teh
triangle(s)	**triángulo(s)** tree-AHN-goo-loh(s)
trim (molding)	**moldura** mol-DOO-rah
trim (to prune)	**podar** poh-DAR
trim (you prune)	**pode** POH-deh
trimmer(s) (gas)	**orilladora(s) de gasolina** oh-ree-yah-DOH-rah(s) deh gah-soh-LEE-nah
	podadora(s) de gasolina poh-dah-DOH-rah(s) deh gah-soh-LEE-nah
trimmer(s) (hand)	**orilladora(s) manual** oh-ree-yah-DOH-rah(s) mahn-WAHL
	podadora(s) manual(es) poh-dah-DOH-rah(s) mahn-WAHL-(es)
trowel(s)	**cuchara(s)** koo-CHA-rah(s)
	llana(s) YAH-nah(s)
	paleta(s) pah-LEH-tah(s)
	palustre(s) pah-LOOS-treh(s)

troweling	**allanado** ah-yah-NAH-doh
truck(s)	**camión (camiones)** kah-mee-OHN (kah-mee-OH-nes)
truck(s) (pickup)	**camioneta(s)** kah-mee-oh-NEH-tah(s)
trunk(s) (tree)	**tronco(s)** TROHN-koh(s)
truss(es)	**armadura(s)** ar-mah-DOO-rah(s)
try (to)	**tratar** trah-TAR
try (you)	**trate** TRAH-teh
T-square	**regla T** REH-glah teh
tuber(s)	**tubérculo(s)** too-BEHR-kooh-loh(s)
Tuesday	**martes** MAR-tehs
tunnel(s)	**túnel(es)** TOO-nel-(es)
turf	**tepe** TEH-peh
Turn off!	**¡Apáguelo!** ah-PAH-geh-loh
turn off (to) (a switch)	**apagar** ah-pah-GAR
turn off (to) (the water)	**cerrar llave de agua** seh-RAR YAH-veh deh AH-gwah

Turn on!	¡Enciéndalo! en-see-EN-dah-loh
turn on (to) (a switch)	**encender** en-sen-DEHR
turn on (to) (the water)	**abrir llave de agua** ah-BREER YAH-veh deh AH-gwah
unblock (to)	**desbloquear** des-bloh-keh-AR
uncle(s)	**tío(s)** TEE-oh(s)
under	**debajo** deh-BAH-ho
underbrush	**maleza** mah-LEH-sah
underground	**subterráneo** soob-teh-RAH-neh-oh
understand (I)	**comprendo** kohm-PREN-doh
	entiendo cn-tee-EN-doh
understand (to)	**comprender** kohm-pren-DEHR
	entender en-tcn-DER
understand (you)	**comprenda** kohm-PREN-dah
	entienda en-tee-EN-dah
underwear	**ropa interior** ROH-pah cen-teh-ree-OR

uneven (irregular)	**irregular** ee-reh-goo-LAR
	no uniforme no oo-nee-FOR-meh
uneven (rough)	**desparejo** des-par-EH-ho
	desigual deh-see-GWAHL
unfair (unjust)	**injusto** een-HOOS-toh
uniform (consistant)	**uniforme** oo-nee-FOR-meh
uniform(s)	**uniforme(s)** oo-nee-FOR-meh(s)
unload (to)	**descargar** des-kar-GAR
unload (you)	**descargue** des-KAR-geh
unlock (to)	**abrir** ah-BREER
unsafe	**inseguro** een-seh-GOO-roh
untie (to)	**desatar** deh-sah-TAR
untie (you)	**desate** deh-SAH-teh
up (above)	**arriba** ah-REE-bah

up here	**aquí arriba**	
	ah-KEE ah-REE-bah	
upstairs	**arriba**	
	ah-REE-bah	
up there	**allí arriba**	
	ah-YEE ah-REE-bah	
use (to)	**usar**	
	oo-SAR	
use (you)	**use**	
	OO-seh	
utility knife	**cuchillo multiusos**	
	koo-CHEE-yoh mool-tee-OO-sohs	
	cuchillo de uso general	
	koo-CHEE-yoh de OO-soh heh-neh-RAHL	
vacation(s)	**vacaoión (vacaciones)**	
	vah-kah-see-OHN (vah-kah-see-OH-nes)	
vacuum (to)	**aspirar**	
	ahs-pee-RAR	
	limplar con aspiradora	
	leem-pee-AR kohn ahs-pee-rah-DOH-rah	
vacuum (you)	**aspire**	
	ahs-PEE-reh	
	limpie con aspiradora	
	LEEM-pee-eh kohn ahs-pee-rah-DOH-rah	
vacuum bag(s)	**bolsa(s) de aspiradora**	
	BOL-sah(s) deh ahs-pee-rah-DOH-rah	
vacuum cleaner(s)	**aspiradora(s)**	
	ahs-pee-rah-DOH-rah(s)	

valley(s)	**valle(s)** VAH-yeh(s)
valley(s) (roof)	**lima hoya(s)** LEE-mah OH-yah(s)
valve(s)	**válvula(s)** VAHL-voo-lah(s)
vapor barrier	**barrera de vapor** bah-REH-rah deh vah-POR
varnish	**barniz** bar-NEES
varnish (to)	**barnizar** bar-nee-SAR
vase(s)	**florero(s)** floh-REH-roh(s)
	jarrón (jarrones) ha-ROHN (ha-ROH-nes)
vegetable(s)	**verdura(s)** vehr-DOO-rah(s)
vent(s) (air)	**respiradero(s)** res-pee-rah-DEH-roh(s)
	ventilación (ventilaciones) ven-tee-lah-see-OHN (ven-tee-lah-see-OH-nes)
ventilation	**ventilación** ven-tee-lah-see-OHN
ventilation system(s)	**sistema(s) de ventilación** sees-TEH-mah(s) deh ven-tee-lah-see-OHN
vertical	**vertical** vehr-tee-KAHL

very	**muy** moo-ee
vest(s)	**chaleco(s)** cha-LEH-koh(s)
vine(s)	**enredadera(s)** en-reh-dah-DEH-rah(s)
	trepadora(s) treh-pah-DOH-rah(s)
vine(s) (grape)	**vid(es)** VEED-(es)
	parra(s) PAH-rah(s)
vineyard(s)	**viñedo(s)** vee-NYEH-doh(s)
	viña(s) VEE-nyah(s)
vinyl	**vinilo** vee-NEE-loh
vise(s)	**torno(s)** TOR-noh(s)
	prensa(s) PREN-sah(s)
	tornillo(s) de banco tor-NEE-yoh(s) deh BAHN-koh
wait (to)	**esperar** es-peh-RAR
Wait here.	**Espere aquí.** es-PEH-reh ah-KEE
walk (to)	**caminar** kah-mee-NAR

walkway(s)	**pasillo(s)** pah-SEE-yoh(s)
	camino(s) kah-MEE-noh(s)
	ruta(s) de peatones ROO-tah(s) deh peh-ah-TOH-nes
wall(s)	**muro(s)** MOO-roh(s)
	pared(es) pah-RED-(es)
wallpaper	**papel tapiz** pah-PEL tah-PEES
	papel de empapelar pah-PEL deh em-pah-peh-LAR
wall tie(s)	**sujetador(es) de pared** su-heh-tah-DOR-(es) deh pah-RED
want (I)	**quiero** kee-EH-roh
want ___?, Do you	**¿Quiere ___?** kee-EH-reh ___
warehouse(s)	**almacén (almacenes)** ahl-mah-SEN (ahl-mah-SEH-nes)
	bodega(s) boh-DEH-gah(s)
warm	**caliente** kah-lee-EN-teh
warm (lukewarm)	**tibio** TEE-bee-oh
warm (to heat up)	**calentar** kah-len-TAR

warning sign(s) (safety/caution signs)	**aviso(s) de precaución** ah-VEE-soh(s) deh pre-kow-see-OHN
	letrero(s) de precaución leh-TREH-roh(s) deh pre-kow-see-OHN
wash (I)	**lavo** LAH-voh
wash (to)	**lavar** lah-VAR
wash (you)	**lave** LAH-veh
wash by hand (to)	**lavar a mano** lah-VAR ah MAH-noh
washcloth(s)	**toallita(s)** toh-ah-YEE-tah(s)
washer(s) (metal/rubber)	**arandela(s)** ah-rahn-DEH-lah(s)
	empaque(s) em-PAH-keh(s)
	rondana(s) rohn-DAH-nah(s)
washing and ironing	**lavado y planchado** lah-VAH-doh ee plahn-CHA-doh
washing machine(s)	**lavadora(s)** lah-vah-DOH-rah(s)
wash the clothes (to)	**lavar la ropa** lah-VAR lah ROH-pah
wash the clothes (you)	**lave la ropa** LAH-veh lah ROH-pah
wasp(s)	**avispa(s)** ah-VEES-pah(s)

wasps nest(s)	**avispero(s)** ah-vees-PEH-roh(s)
waste (rubbish/trash)	**desechos** deh-SEH-chos
wastepaper basket(s)	**cesto(s) de basura** SES-toh(s) deh bah-SOO-rah
	bote(s) de basura BOH-teh(s) deh bah-SOO-rah
watch (to)	**mirar** mee-RAR
Watch me.	**Míreme.** MEE-reh-meh
Watch out!	**¡Cuidado!** kwee-DAH-doh
water	**agua** AH-gwah
water (to)	**regar** reh-GAR
water heater(s)	**calentador(es) de agua** kah-len-tah-DOR-(es) deh AH-gwah
watering zone(s)	**zona(s) de riego** SOH-nah(s) deh ree-EH-goh
wax	**cera** SEH-rah
wax (to)	**encerar** en-seh-RAR
wear (to) (clothing)	**llevar puesto** yeh-VAR PWES-toh
	ponerse poh-NEHR-seh

wear (you) (clothing)	**lleve puesto** YEH-veh PWES-toh
	póngase POHN-gah-seh
weather	**tiempo** tee-EM-poh
weather (bad)	**mal tiempo** mahl tee-EM-poh
weather (good)	**buen tiempo** bwen tee-EM-poh
weather strip	**junta hermética** HOON-tah ehr-MEH-tee-kah
wedge(s)	**cuña(s)** KOO-nyah(s)
	caiza(s) KAHL-sah(s)
Wednesday	**miércoles** mee-EHR-koh-les
weed (to)	**deshierbar** des-ee-ehr-BAR
	sacar las hierbas malas sah-KAR lahs ee-EHR-bahs MAH-lahs
	escardar es-kar-DAR
weed (you)	**deshierbe** des-ee-EHR-beh
	saque las hierbas malas SAH-keh lahs ee-EHR-bahs MAH-lahs
	escarde es-KAR-deh

weed control	**control de malezas** kohn-TROL deh mah-LEH-sahs
weeds	**hierbas malas** ee-EHR-bahs MAH-lahs
	malezas mah-LEH-sahs
weed trimmer(s)	**orilladora(s)** oh-ree-yah-DOH-rah(s)
	cortadora(s) de hierbas malas kor-tah-DOH-rah(s) deh ee-EHR-bahs MAH-lahs
week(s)	**semana(s)** seh-MAH-nah(s)
weekend(s)	**fin(es) de semana** FEEN-(es) deh seh-MAH-nah
weekly	**semanal** seh-mah-NAHL
weigh (to)	**pesar** peh-SAR
weight	**peso** PEH-soh
well done (good job)	**muy bien** moo-ee be-en
west	**oeste** oh-ES-teh
wet	**mojado** moh-HA-doh
wet (to)	**mojar** moh-HAR
What?	**¿Qué?** keh

wheel(s)	**rueda(s)**
	roo-EH-dah(s)
wheelbarrow(s)	**carretilla(s)**
	kah-reh-TEE-yah(s)
When?	**¿Cuándo?**
	KWAHN-doh
Where?	**¿Dónde?**
	DOHN-deh
whiskbroom(s)	**escobilla(s)**
	es-koh-BEE-yah(s)
white	**blanco**
	BLAHN-koh
whitefly	**mosca blanca**
	MOHS-kah BLAHN-kah
Who?	**¿Quién?**
	kee-EN
whole (entire)	**todo**
	TOH-doh
Why?	**¿Por que?**
	por KEH
wide	**ancho**
	AHN-cho
width	**anchura**
	ahn-CHOO-rah
wife (wives)	**esposa(s)**
	es-POH-sah(s)
wind (breeze)	**viento**
	vee-EN-toh
window(s)	**ventana(s)**
	ven-TAH-nah(s)

window casing(s)	**marco(s) de ventana** MAR-koh(s) deh ven-TAH-nah
windowsill(s)	**solera(s) de la ventana** soh-LEH-rah(s) deh lah ven-TAH-nah
	alféizar(es) ahl-FEH-sar-(es)
winter	**invierno** een-vee-EHR-noh
wire(s)	**alambre(s)** ah-LAHM-breh(s)
wire (to install wiring)	**instalar el cableado** eens-tah-LAR el kah-bleh-AH-doh
wire brush(es)	**cepillo(s) de alambre** seh-PEE-yoh(s) deh ah-LAHM-breh
wire cutter(s)	**cortador(es) de alambre** kor-tah-DOR-(es) deh ah-LAHM-breh
wiring	**cableado** kah-bleh-AH-doh
with	**con** kohn
without	**sin** seen
woman (women)	**mujer(es)** moo-HEHR-(es)
wood	**madera** mah-DEH-rah
wooden	**de madera** deh mah-DEH-rah
wood filler	**relleno de madera** reh-YEH-noh deh mah-DEH-rah

wood stain(s)	**tinte(s) para madera** TEEN-teh(s) PAH-rah mah-DEH-rah
word(s)	**palabra(s)** pah-LAH-brah(s)
work	**trabajo** trah-BAH-ho
work (to)	**trabajar** trah-bah-HAR
work bench	**banco de trabajo** BAHN-koh deh trah-BAH-ho
work clothes	**ropa de trabajo** ROH-pah deh trah-BAH-ho
worker(s)	**trabajador(es)** trah-bah-ha-DOR-(es) **obrero(s)** oh-BREH-roh(s)
workers' compensation insurance	**seguro de compensación por accidentes de trabajo** seh-GOO-roh deh kohm-pen-sah see-OHN por ahk-see-DEN-tes de trah-BAH-ho
worm(s)	**lombriz (lombrices)** lohm-BREES (lohm-BREE-ses) **gusano(s)** goo-SAH-noh(s)
wound(s)	**herida(s)** eh-REE-dah(s)
wrench(es)	**llave(s) de tuercas** YAH-veh(s) deh TWEHR-kahs
wrist(s)	**muñeca(s)** moo-NYEH-kah(s)
write (to)	**escribir** es-kree-BEER

write (you)	**escriba** es-KREE-bah
written contract(s)	**contrato(s) por escrito** kohn-TRAH-toh(s) por es-KREE-toh
wrong (bad)	**malo** MAH-loh
wrong (incorrect)	**incorrecto** een-koh-REK-toh
yard(s) (garden)	**jardín (jardines)** har-DEEN (har-DEE-nes)
	patio(s) PAH-tee-oh(s)
yard(s) (measurement)	**yarda(s)** YAR-dah(s)
yard waste	**desechos de jardín** deh-SEH-chos deh har-DEEN
year(s)	**año(s)** AH-nyoh(s)
yellow	**amarillo** ah-mah-REE-yoh
yes	**sí** see
yesterday	**ayer** ah-YEHR
you	**usted** oo-STED
zip code(s)	**código(s) postal(es)** KOH-dee-goh(s) pohs-TAHL-(es)
zone(s)	**zona(s)** SOH-nah(s)